For Arthur – there's more to the world than meets the eye – C.S.

For the Abadia family, my stars – X.A.

BIG PICTURE PRESS

First published in the UK in 2021 by Big Picture Press,
an imprint of Bonnier Books UK,
4th Floor, Victoria House, Bloomsbury Square, London, WC1B 4DA
Owned by Bonnier Books, Sveavägen 56, Stockholm, Sweden
www.templarco.co.uk/big-picture-press
www.bonnierbooks.co.uk

1 3 5 7 9 10 8 6 4 2

MIX
Paper from
responsible sources
FSC® C018236
FSC
www.fsc.org

ISBN 978-1-78741-642-0

This book was typeset in Ulissa, BSKombat, Anne Bonny and VAG-HandWritten.
The illustrations were created with graphite,
wax and ink, and coloured digitally.

Consulted by Dr Nathan Adams
Edited by Carly Blake and Joanna McInerney
Designed by Adam Allori and Olivia Cook
Production by Neil Randles

Printed in Poland

The
STARDUST
THAT MADE US

Written by **COLIN STUART**

Illustrated by **XIMO ABADÍA**

BPP

WHERE DID IT ALL COME FROM?

GROUPS

PEOPLE AND PLACES

EVERYDAY LIFE

THE FUTURE

The Extraordinary Elements

The Universe is an extraordinary place filled with awe and wonder. Stars twinkle, flowers bloom and animals run, fly and swim as we humans go about our busy lives. Yet even the most ordinary objects have a hidden beauty deep within.

The secret lies in what makes it all work. **Nature has an unseen cookbook full of recipes for making everything you've ever encountered**, from fish to fingernails, sand to Saturn. But what are the ingredients? Scientists call them ELEMENTS and we currently know of 118 different ones. Some you will have heard of, like iron and oxygen. Others you probably haven't, like praseodymium and dysprosium. Elements are combined in different ways to make different things. Red blood cells, for example, combine oxygen, hydrogen, nitrogen, iron and carbon to carry oxygen around your body.

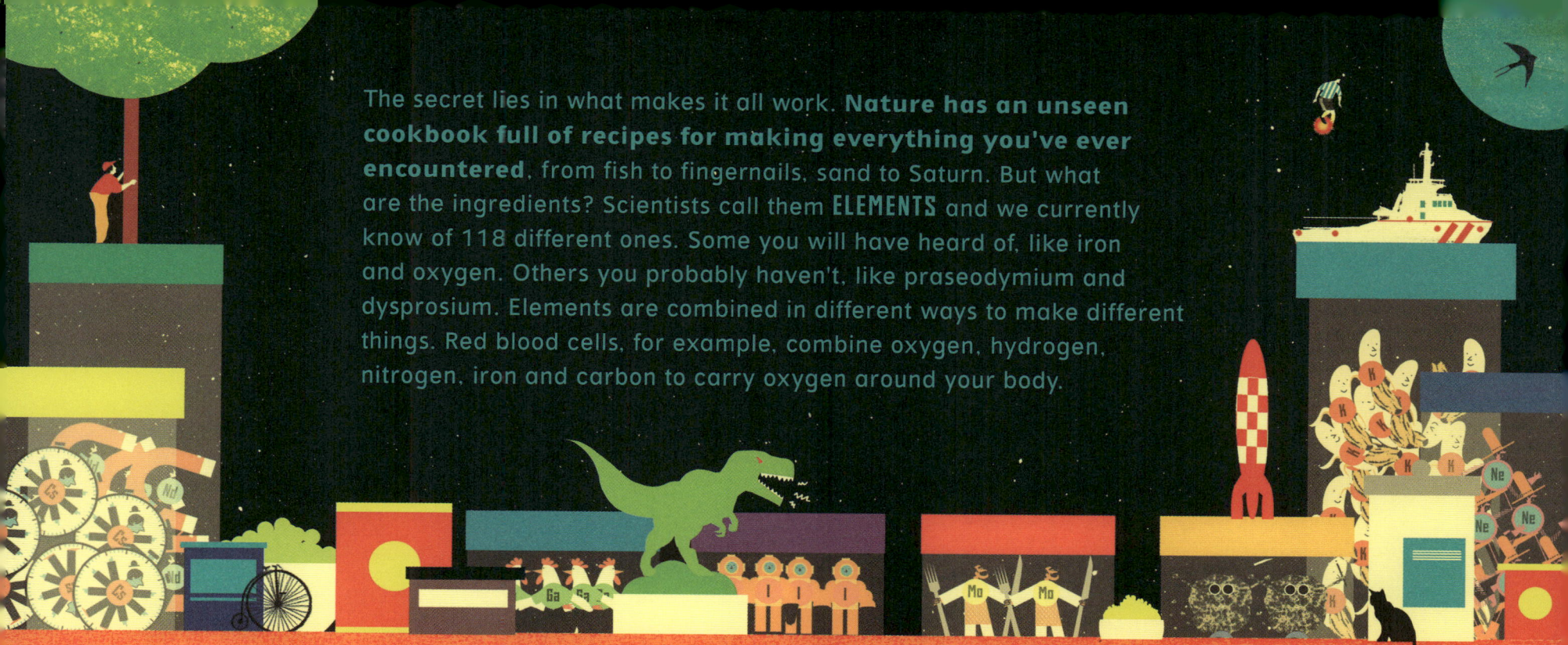

Each element has a personality of its own, behaving in a unique way that makes it distinct from every other. It has taken centuries of effort by scientists around the world to uncover them all. Often scientists have gone to great lengths to find a new element – one was discovered by boiling urine (page 37), while others only appeared once we had huge machines to smash particles together at close to the speed of light (page 75). All of them are special and we use many of them every day without even realising.

This is the story of the extraordinary elements. Welcome to the world of chemistry!

Elements Basics

All around you, every day of your life, there are tiny **invisible particles** doing extraordinary things. Everything you can touch, taste, see or smell is made up of **ATOMS**. In the **centre of an atom are particles called PROTONS** and **NEUTRONS**, with even lighter electrons journeying around them.

The **number of protons an atom has** is really important. Scientists call this the ATOMIC NUMBER. If every atom in a material has the same atomic number then we call it an element. A bar of gold weighing 12.4 kilograms for example, is made up of 38 trillion trillion atoms and each and every one has 79 protons in it. If you had the same number of atoms but with 47 protons in each atom, then you would have a bar of silver instead. Today, scientists know of elements with atomic numbers from 1 all the way up to 118.

If a MOLECULE, a small group of atoms, is made of more than one element then the material is called a COMPOUND. For example, you breathe out carbon dioxide (CO_2) – a compound made of one atom of carbon linked to two atoms of oxygen. The same compound is taken in by plants.

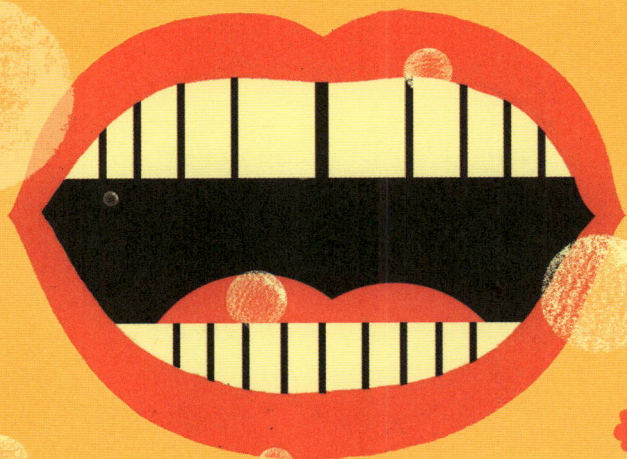

Let's Talk Chemistry

Scientists who study the elements and the way they behave and co-operate to form new substances are called **CHEMISTS**. The subject they study is known as chemistry.

nucleus

electrons

A lot of chemistry boils down to the electrons whizzing around inside atoms. All atoms have a nucleus at their centre, which is surrounded by rings called shells, It is inside these shells, that we find **ELECTRONS** – **tiny, negatively-charged particles orbiting around the nucleus at impossible speeds**. Each shell can only hold a certain number of electrons.

An atom is happiest (chemically stable) when its outer shell is full of electrons and there are different ways it can achieve this. In **IONIC BONDING, an atom can donate a few electrons to another that is missing some, which causes them to cling together**. This happens when a sodium atom lends a chlorine atom an electron, forming sodium chloride, or table salt.

SODIUM

CHLORINE

SODIUM CHLORIDE

In **COVALENT BONDING, atoms end up sharing electrons so that they both have complete outer shells.** Take a molecule of water, for example. Its chemical symbol is H_2O – two atoms of hydrogen bonded to one atom of oxygen. An atom of hydrogen has a single electron in its outer shell and an atom of oxygen has six. In a water molecule, the electrons from the two hydrogen atoms are shared to give oxygen a full outer shell of eight electrons.

WATER MOLECULE [H_2O]

Mendeleev

Have you ever been to the zoo? It's amazing to see all the creatures that make up the animal kingdom and the differences in the way they look and behave. Over centuries of study, biologists have worked out how the animals fit into groups. Lions and tigers are both members of the cat family. Horses and zebras belong together too.

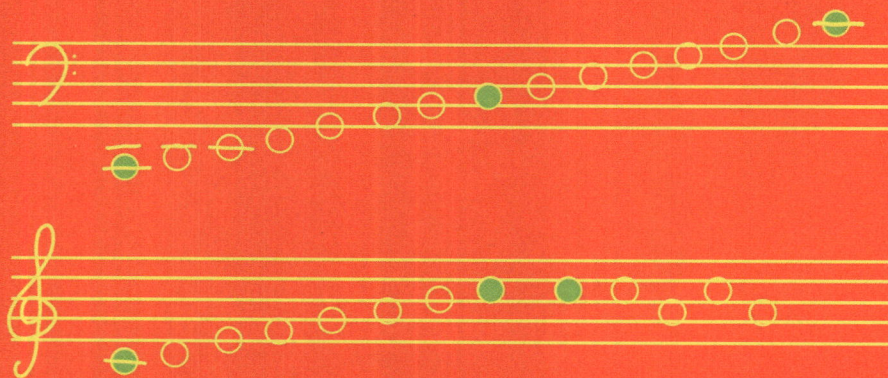

As chemists began to find new elements in the 1600s they also started to put them into groups based on properties they had in common. By the 1860s more than 50 elements had been discovered and the English chemist JOHN NEWLANDS spotted a pattern. **If you organised the known elements by atomic number then every eighth one shared similar properties**, just like the eighth note of an octave in music. This became known as THE LAW OF OCTAVES.

DMITRI MENDELEEV soon stepped in to continue investigations. In 1869, the Russian chemist had a dream in which he saw the **elements arranged into a table according to patterns in their behaviour.** As these behaviours repeat periodically (in a regular way), it became known as THE PERIODIC TABLE. Mendeleev woke from his dream and hastily scribbled down the first ever periodic table on a piece of paper. It contained all 63 elements known at the time.

MENDELEEV'S PERIODIC TABLE ADAPTED, 1871

I	II	III	IV	V	VI	VII	VIII		
H									
Li	Be	B	C	N	O	F			
Na	Mg	Al	Si	P	S	Cl			
K	Ca		Ti	V	Cr	Mn	Fe	Co	Ni
Cu	Zn			As	Se	Br			
Rb	Sr	Y	Zr	Nb	Mo		Ru	Rh	Pd
Ag	Cd	In	Sn	Sb	Te	I			
Cs	Ba	Di	Ce				Os	Ir	Pt
		Er	La	Ta	W				
Au	Hg	Tl	Pb	Bi					
		Th		U					

?

One of the clever things about Mendeleev's table is that it had gaps. Observing the patterns, he correctly guessed that new elements yet to be discovered belonged in these spaces. It was even possible to predict their properties based on their position in the repeating pattern. Later, the elements germanium, gallium and scandium were found, and the gaps were filled in.

scientists know of so far. The table **organises the elements into a grid and the different sections tell us more about how each element behaves**. Each square represents one element. The colours of the squares show elements with similar properties. For example, the green squares show the metalloids.

Vertical columns in the table are called **GROUPS**. They start with group 1 on the far left and end with group 18 on the far right. The elements in a group often look and behave similarly, because **they have the same number of electrons in their outermost shell**. Some of them have peculiar names like the pnictogens (group 15).

Horizontal rows are known as **PERIODS**. There are seven in total. **All the elements in a period have the same number of electron shells.** The most metallic elements are at the left end of a period and the least metallic on the far right end. The size of the atom goes down as you move along a period from left to right. There are so many elements in two periods – the lanthanides and the actinides – that they are moved to the bottom to stop the table becoming too wide.

	1	2	3	4	5	6	7	8
1	1 Hydrogen							
2	3 Lithium	4 Beryllium						
3	11 Sodium	12 Magnesium						
4	19 Potassium	20 Calcium	21 Scandium	22 Titanium	23 Vanadium	24 Chromium	25 Manganese	26 Iron
5	37 Rubidium	38 Strontium	39 Yttrium	40 Zirconium	41 Niobium	42 Molybdenum	43 Technetium	44 Ruthenium
6	55 Caesium	56 Barium	57–71	72 Hafnium	73 Tantalum	74 Tungsten	75 Rhenium	76 Osmium
7	87 Francium	88 Radium	89–103	104 Rutherfordium	105 Dubnium	106 Seaborgium	107 Bohrium	108 Hassium

LANTHANIDES

57 Lanthanum	58 Cerium	59 Praseodymium	60 Neodymium	61 Promethium	62 Samarium

ACTINIDES

89 Actinium	90 Thorium	91 Protactinium	92 Uranium	93 Neptunium	94 Plutonium

16

KEY

86 Rn Radon

Each element's square is packed full of information about the element, including its **chemical symbol** (centre) and **atomic number** (top left). Some versions also show the atomic weight and even the number of electrons in each shell surrounding the element's nucleus.

The **weight of the atom increases as you move down a group** from top to bottom.

13	14	15	16	17	18
					2 He Helium
5 B Boron	6 C Carbon	7 N Nitrogen	8 O Oxygen	9 F Fluorine	10 Ne Neon
13 Al Aluminium	14 Si Silicon	15 P Phosphorus	16 S Sulphur	17 Cl Chlorine	18 Ar Argon

9	10	11	12						
Co Cobalt	28 Ni Nickel	29 Cu Copper	30 Zi Zinc	31 Ga Gallium	32 Ge Germanium	33 As Arsenic	34 Se Selenium	35 Br Bromine	36 Kr Krypton
Rh Rhodium	46 Pd Palladium	47 Ag Silver	48 Cd Cadmium	49 In Indium	50 Sn Tin	51 Sb Antimony	52 Te Tellurium	53 I Iodine	54 Xe Xenon
Ir Iridium	78 Pt Platinum	79 Au Gold	80 Hg Mercury	81 Tl Thallium	82 Pb Lead	83 Bi Bismuth	84 Po Polonium	85 At Astatine	86 Rn Radon
Mt eitnerium	110 Ds Darmstadtium	111 Rg Roentgenium	112 Cr Copernicium	113 Nh Nihonium	114 Fl Flerovium	115 Mc Moscovium	116 Lu Livermorium	117 Ts Tennessine	118 Og Oganesson

Eu uropium	64 Gd Gadolinium	65 Tb Terbium	66 Dy Dyspros um	67 Ho Holmium	68 Er Erbium	69 Tm Thulium	70 Yb Ytterbium	71 Lu Lutetium
Rm mericium	96 Cm Curium	97 Bk Berkelium	98 Cf Californ um	99 Es Einsteinium	100 Fm Fermium	101 Md Mendelevium	102 No Nobelium	103 Lr Lawrencium

The Big Bang

In the beginning there were no elements at all. **Our Universe exploded into existence in a sea of energy** nearly 14 billion years ago in an event called **THE BIG BANG**. In the first millionth of a second, some of that energy was turned into protons and electrons. For the first time, the ingredients for hydrogen (H) – the earliest element – existed.

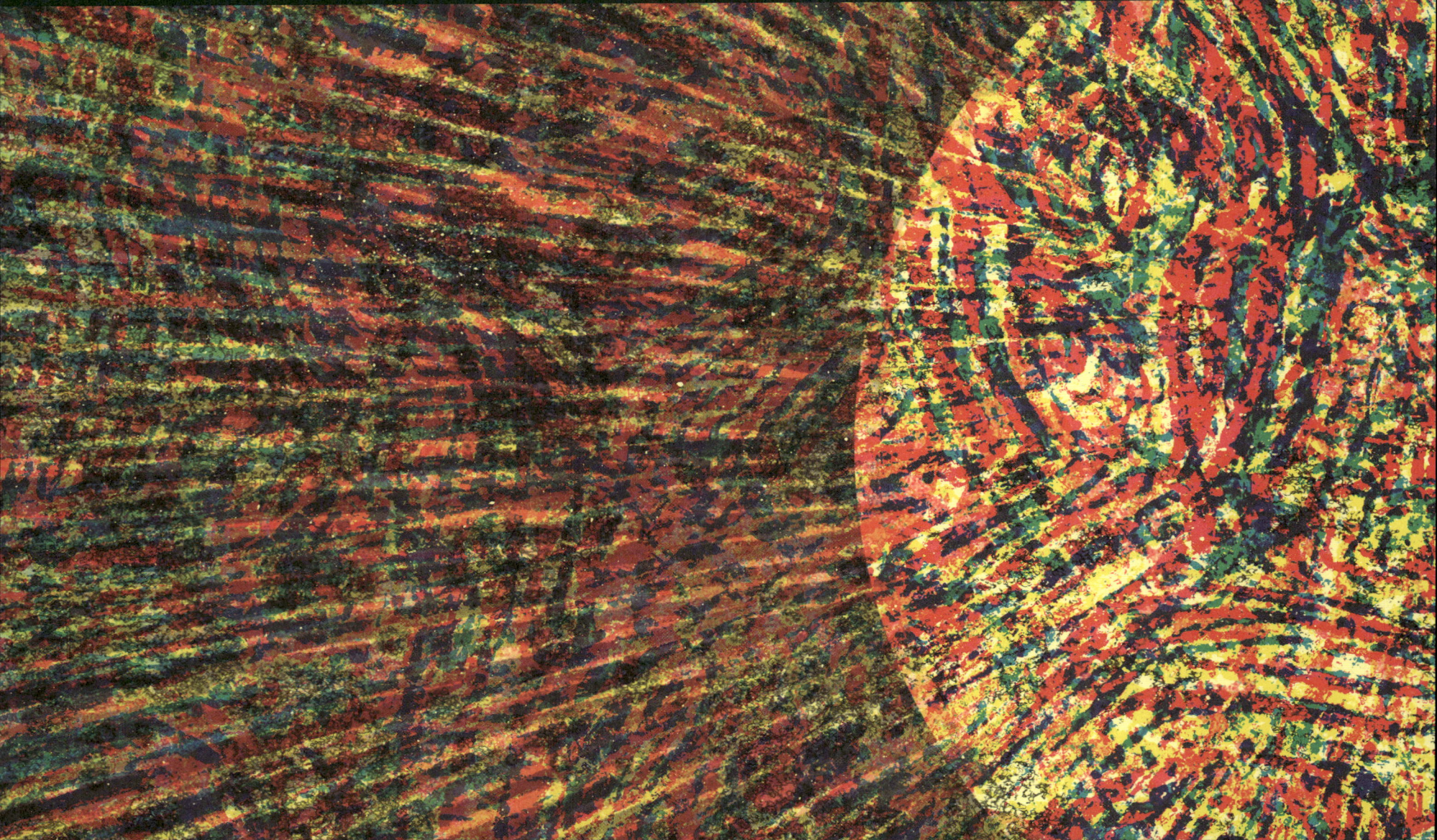

When the Universe was just three minutes old, **protons started bumping into each other and sticking together in a process called FUSION**. The next three elements were made: Helium (He), and tiny amounts of lithium (Li) and beryllium (Be). Fusion stopped 20 minutes after the Big Bang and no new elements were made for a long time. The Universe was now 75 per cent hydrogen and 25 per cent helium.

After the initial 17-minute burst of fusion following the Big Bang, it was hundreds of millions of years before any of the other elements of the periodic table began to appear. The Universe kept expanding and getting cooler, meaning there was less and less energy in each piece of space. It would take something remarkable to turn the Universe into an element-making factory again: the birth of the very first stars.

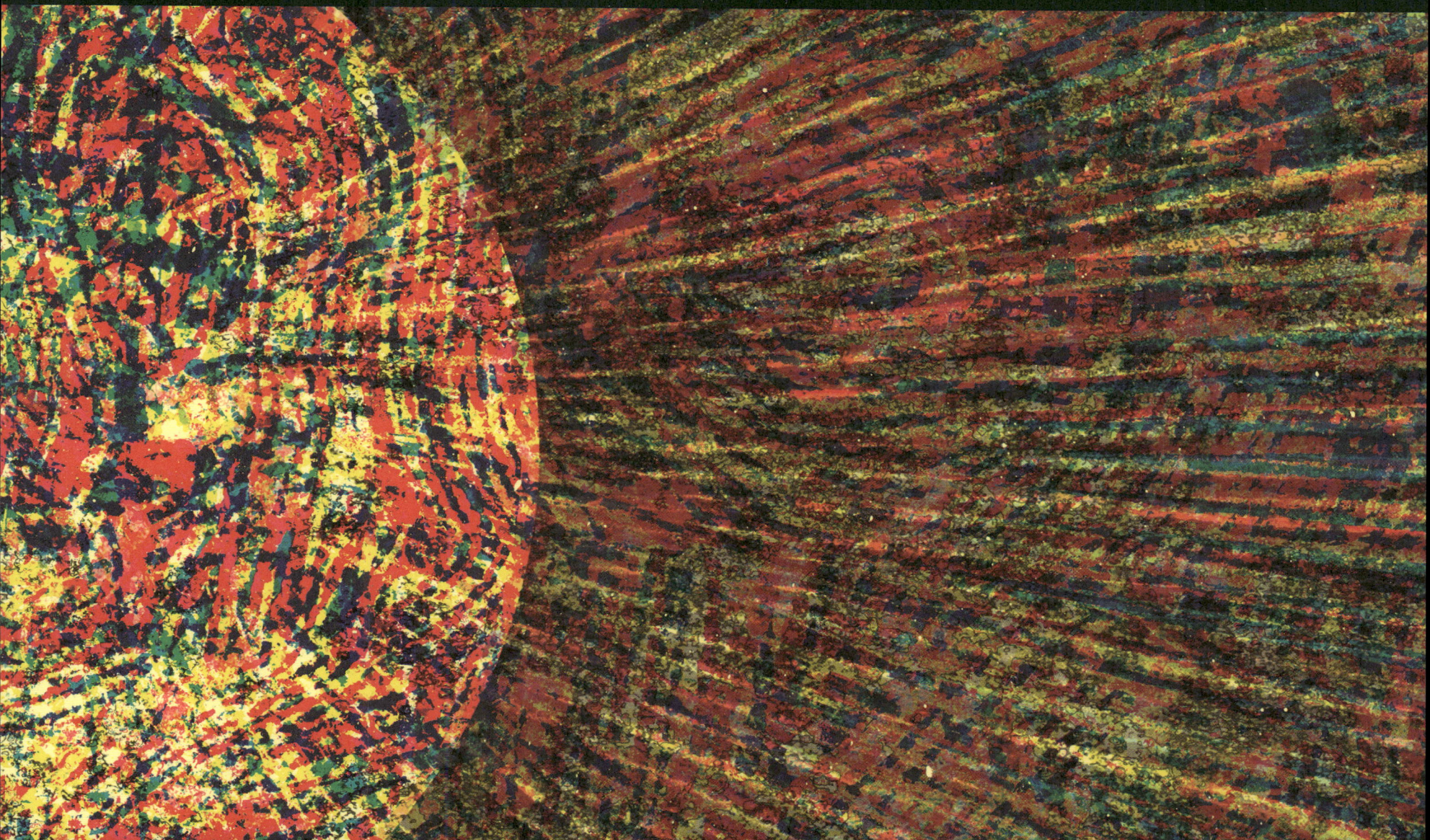

All of the findings made by astronomers and scientists up until now tell us the Big Bang happened – but it remains a theory and theories need evidence to back them up. The percentages of the first two elements, hydrogen and helium, are an excellent test. If astronomers found a Universe with hugely different amounts of hydrogen and helium, it would make them doubt whether the Big Bang really happened. Yet, when we look around the Universe we see that it is still mostly 75 per cent hydrogen and 25 per cent helium. This is almost exactly what the Sun consists of too.

The Stardust That Made Us

Stars are colossal balls of hot material shining brightly in space. Today, we estimate there are nearly one septillion stars (one with 24 zeroes after it) in the Universe. However, the very first stars only lit up the cosmos a few hundred million years after the Big Bang.

gravity

fusion

Stars contain so much stuff that gravity crushes in on their cores with an unimaginable force. These conditions are perfect for fusion – the same process that turned hydrogen into helium just after the Big Bang (page 18). Turning hydrogen into helium is exactly what most stars do. The energy fusion creates pushes back against gravity, making sure the star doesn't collapse in on itself.

THE CNO CYCLE

nitrogen + hydrogen = helium + carbon

6

oxygen - positron - neutrino = nitrogen

5

nitrogen + hydrogen = oxygen + gamma ray

4

KEY

+	**POSITRON**	A positively charged particle. Positrons are the antiparticles of electrons.
⌇	**GAMMA RAY**	The most energetic form of light.
V	**NEUTRINO**	Tiny particles with a neutral charge.

1

carbon + hydrogen = nitrogen + gamma ray

2

nitrogen – neutrino – positron = carbon

3

carbon + hydrogen = nitrogen + gamma ray

Stars 1.5 times more massive than the Sun primarily **fuse hydrogen into helium** through six steps using carbon (C), nitrogen (N) and oxygen (O). Astronomers call this the **CNO CYCLE** and German physicists **CARL FRIEDRICH VON WEIZSÄCKER** and **HANS BETHE** proposed its secrets in the 1930s. Most of the carbon and nitrogen in the Universe was made inside the core of stars as they grew old. In fact, the four most abundant elements in your body (oxygen, carbon, hydrogen and nitrogen) were all made inside huge star explosions, meaning you are very much made of stardust.

Fusion is how our own Sun makes the energy we receive as sunlight. Play in the park on a sunny day and you are bathing in the light of a giant nuclear reactor 150 million kilometres away. The Sun fuses 620 million tonnes of hydrogen every single second. However, the Sun is too small to achieve the CNO cycle of fusion reactions that creates a heavier set of elements.

Dying Stars

Dying stars are the ultimate element-making machines. They play a big part in creating a whole host of other elements including lithium, barium, tin, mercury, cadmium and strontium.

Stars begin to die when their fuel runs out and fusion stops. The most massive stars run out of fuel within ten million years. When fusion stops, gravity wins and the star's core collapses, sending a huge shockwave surging out through the rest of the star. It is so powerful that it tears the star apart in **a violent explosion called a SUPERNOVA**. Many familiar elements, including oxygen (O), neon (Ne), aluminium (Al), chlorine (Cl), sodium (Na) and magnesium (Mg), were made inside exploding stars.

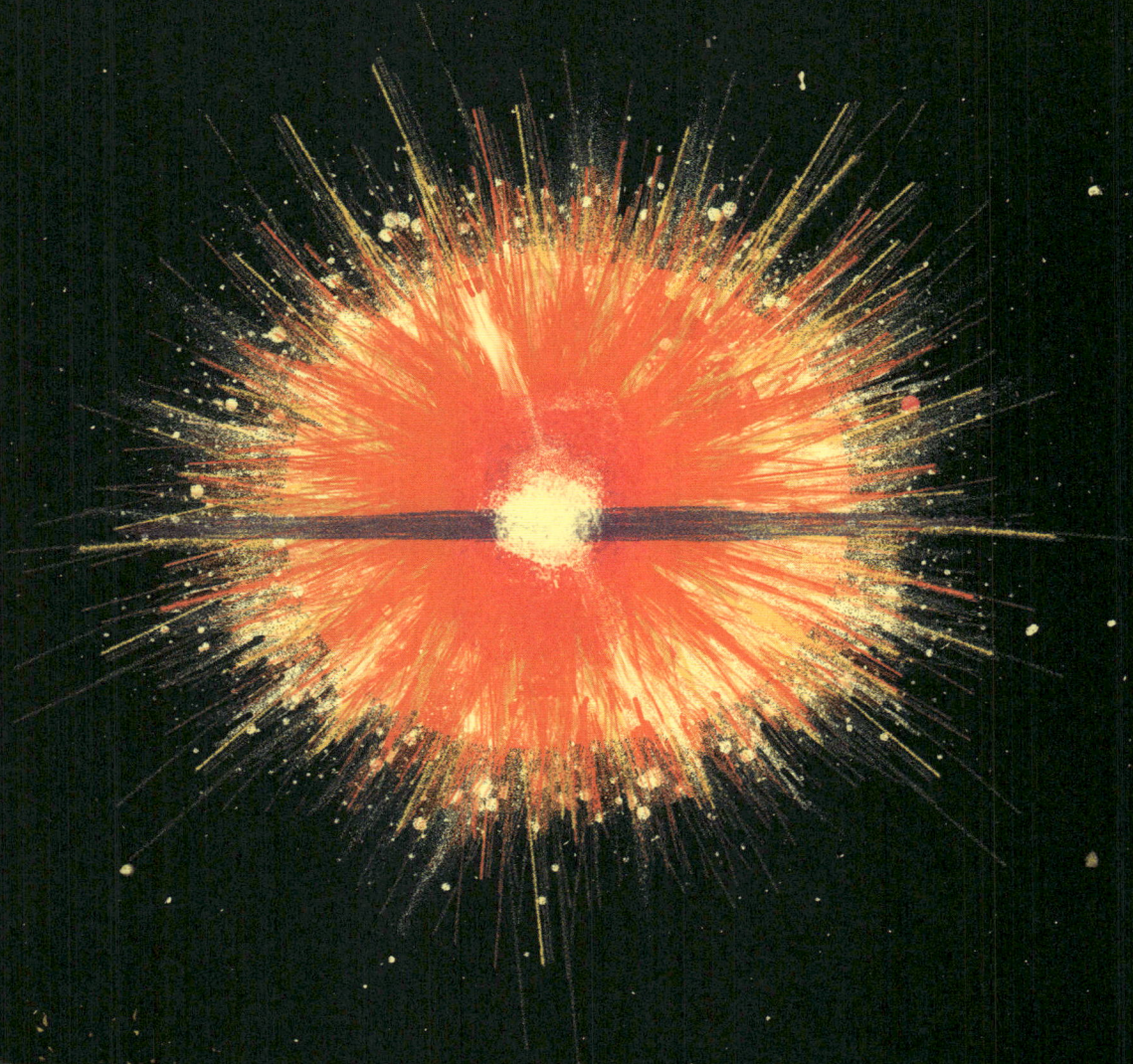

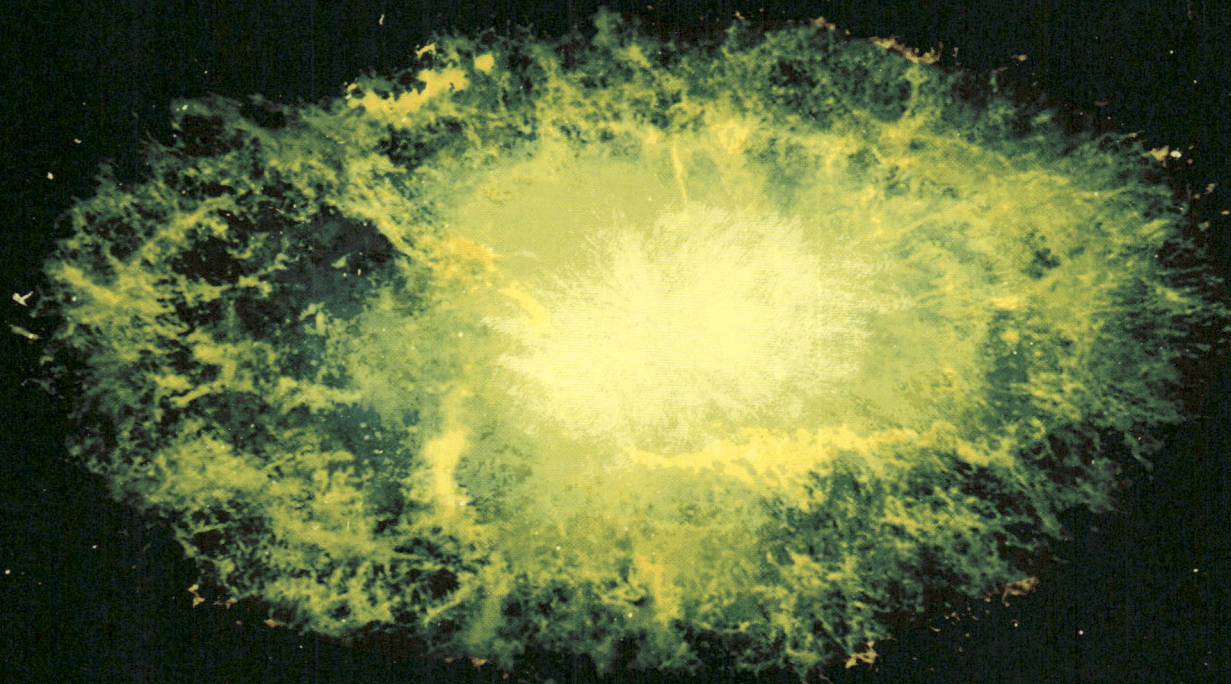

The force of a supernova sends material flying across the Universe, which mixes with elements from other dead stars to form **giant clouds called NEBULAE**. When nebulae become too heavy, they collapse to form new stars and solar systems.

There is another explosive way that stars can make new elements. When our Sun eventually dies, its core will become a **WHITE DWARF** – **a super-dense Earth-sized object mostly made of carbon (C)**. The gravitational pull of a white dwarf is so strong that it can steal material from a nearby star, making itself heavier and heavier.

SUN

WHITE DWARF

Eventually the white dwarf gets so heavy that it also explodes. Most of the Universe's titanium (Ti), iron (Fe), nickel (Ni) and copper (Cu) was made during white dwarf detonations. But stars much bigger than the Sun leave behind something even more exotic when they die: a neutron star.

NEARBY STAR

Star Sparkle

Neutron stars are so extreme it's difficult to contemplate – they have some of the strongest gravitational and magnetic fields in the Universe. Imagine crushing half of the Sun (which could fit 1.3 million Earths inside it) down into a ball the size of London or Paris. A neutron star is so heavy that a single teaspoon of its material weighs more than every person on Earth put together. It spins hundreds of times every second and is so highly magnetised that it spits beams of energy from its poles. That's why astronomers sometimes refer to them as the Universe's lighthouses.

More often than not, stars live in pairs. If both stars die and become neutron stars then they can become locked into a dizzying death spiral. When they smash together with unimaginable force, new elements are made. Almost every element from rubidium (Rb, atomic number 37) to plutonium (Pu, atomic number 94) in the periodic table was made this way, including the precious metals gold (Au), silver (Ag) and platinum (Pt).

Gold is prized for its attractive colour and shininess. It is also the most **MALLEABLE** of all the metals – that means **it is easy to shape** into different things, from necklaces and earrings to bracelets and rings. But like all precious metals, gold is rare. The total amount of gold in the world, not including any yet to be found, is nearly 200,000 tonnes. It would all fit inside a 21-metre cube.

Precious metals are often used to make jewellery. If you own anything made of these elements, then you are holding the smashed up pieces of colliding neutron stars in the palm of your hand.

A single cosmic crash creates enough gold to match the weight of 200 Earths. The same event creates 500 Earth's worth of platinum.

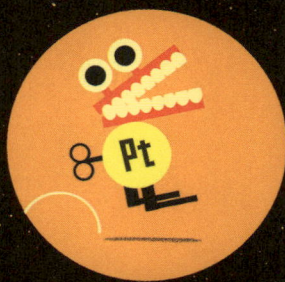

x200

x500

Maybe you are wondering why diamond doesn't appear on the periodic table? Diamond is actually a form of highly compressed carbon (C). In 2014, scientists discovered what they believe to be the coldest white dwarf star ever studied. Its carbon centre had crystallised, forming a diamond the size of Earth.

Human-Made

For billions of years only the Universe was capable of making new elements. But of the current 118 entries in the periodic table, 26 elements are SYNTHETIC – they were **made by scientists during their experiments.**

Element number 43 was one of the gaps Mendeleev predicted (see p15) but scientists struggled for decades to find it. Then, in 1937, CARLO PERRIER and EMILIO SEGRÈ created it by firing **tiny particles** called DEUTERONS at the element molybdenum (Mo, atomic number 42). As it was the first element to be created using technology, it was called technetium (Tc). Other elements, including neptunium (Np), plutonium (Pu) and americium (Am), are made in a similar way inside nuclear reactors.

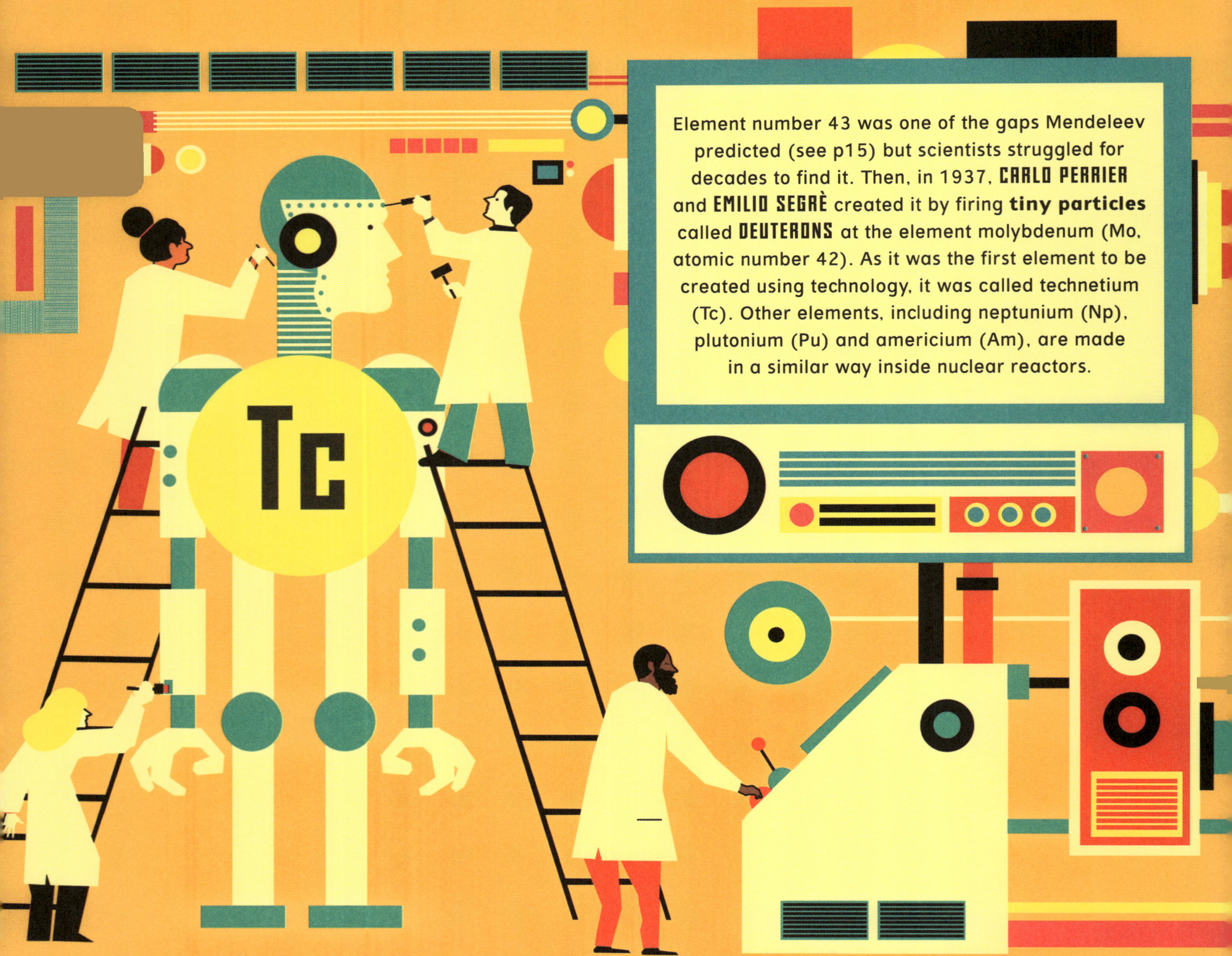

Tc

No stable versions of human-made elements occur naturally on Earth, so scientists know relatively little about most of them. Most have only ever existed as a few atoms for a fraction of a second in a lab before breaking down. The atoms of most synthetic elements are huge compared to those at the beginning of the periodic table.

Making these elements is incredibly difficult and time-consuming. Aiming the particles at the target is a hard thing to get right – a bit like trying to throw marshmallows into someone's mouth. You won't be successful every time. That makes synthetic elements very rare and expensive.

Each gram of californium (Cf), for example, costs $27 million to make, but it has some valuable uses, including detecting gold and silver in ore.

New elements used to be discovered by lone scientists toiling away in their labs. The latest additions to the periodic table took hundreds of researchers, working right around the world, years to find. All because we never know what uses new elements could have in the future...

Alkali Metals

The clever thing about the periodic table is that it organises the elements into sets depending on the way they behave. **All six elements in the first column of the table (except for hydrogen) are known as ALKALI METALS.** Their atoms have a single electron in their outer shell which they will lose easily – and this makes all of the six alkali metals highly reactive.

When you think of the word 'metal' what other words come to mind? Heavy? Strong? Tough? Not all metals are like that. The alkali metals are soft and light. It is possible to cut through lithium (Li), sodium (Na) and potassium (K) with a knife. Lithium is the lightest metal and it has a similar density to pinewood.

You may have heard of the Bunsen burner, but did you know that the German chemist who invented it back in 1855 also discovered two alkali metals? Using the burner and another of his inventions called a spectroscope, ROBERT BUNSEN heated elements and observed that they each give off a different light, which led to the discovery of rubidium (Rb) and caesium (Cs). Both elements are very reactive and can ignite in air.

Caesium plays a crucial role in your everyday life as a very accurate timekeeper. Caesium clocks are used to keep time in mobile phones and GPS satellites. Without caesium, you would get lost much more often!

Officially a second lasts for as long as it takes for a caesium-133 atom to change in a certain way a total of 9,192,631,770 (nine billion, one hundred and ninety-two million, six hundred and thirty-one thousand, seven hundred and seventy-one) times.

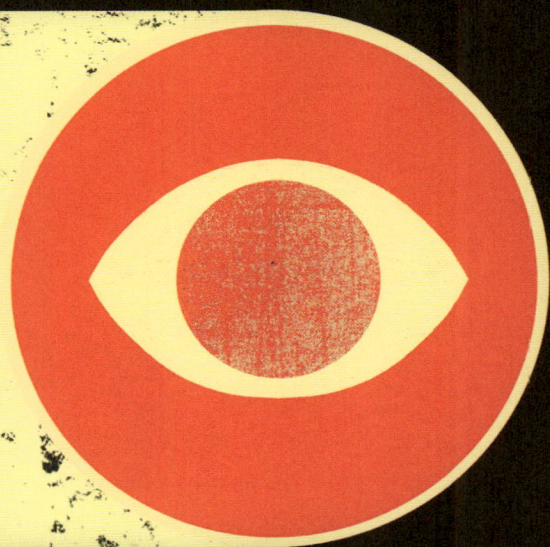

Alkaline Earth Metals

The second column of the periodic table is home to **six shiny, silvery-white elements** known collectively as the **ALKALINE EARTH METALS**. Some are vital to your existence — such as the calcium found in your bones — but, like their neighbours the alkali metals, others are downright dangerous.

Radium (Ra) was famously discovered by **MARIE CURIE** and gets its name from the rays it releases. It is highly **RADIOACTIVE**, meaning it **releases energy via radiation that is harmful to humans**. We didn't always know that, though. Around 100 years ago we added it to toothpaste, hair creams and even food! Radium was also once used to make the hands on watches glow in the dark.

Hair Cream

Toothpaste

There are only eight elements more abundant in the Universe than magnesium (Mg). On Earth, you'll find a lot of this element in seawater. It's an essential ingredient needed by every cell in your body to make them function properly. Plants also need it to make **CHLOROPHYLL** – the **green pigment important in photosynthesis.**

Beryllium (Be) gets its name from the mineral beryl, which we've been using since at least the days of ancient Egypt to make gemstones including emeralds.

The element is particularly good for making the mirrors that are used in weather satellites and space telescopes. In space, temperatures can change from hot to cold very quickly, causing mirrors to expand and contract. Beryllium mirrors expand and contract very little, and so keep their shape better than glass ones.

Most of the beryllium on Earth is made when **highly energised particles from space called COSMIC RAYS** rain down on our planet and hit atoms in our atmosphere. When the Sun has lots of solar storms it stops as many cosmic rays hitting Earth and so the amount of beryllium being created in the atmosphere also drops. Scientists have studied ice cores – long, thin columns dug down into permafrost in Antarctica – to measure the changing amounts of beryllium over time. It allows astronomers to study the Sun's activity over the last 10,000 years.

Transition Metals

The largest collection of elements makes up a third of the periodic table. They are known as the TRANSITION METALS. **This group of elements are all very hard, with high melting points and boiling points**. Tungsten (W), for example, is exceptionally strong and has the highest melting point of any metal at 3422°C.

Manganese (Mn) is important in construction – the compound manganese oxide is used in making cement and manganese is added to steel (an alloy of iron and carbon) to make it easier to shape into thin sheets. The transition metal molybdenum (Mo) is also used in steel production to fight corrosion.

We've been using some transition metals for a very long time. Some ancient cave paintings in France were made using black paint containing the element manganese.

Element 76, Osmium (Os) is the densest naturally occurring element in the periodic table. As well as being used in pacemakers and heart valves, Osmium is also used to help catch criminals. The compound osmium tetroxide reacts with the oil on skin left behind when someone has touched an object with their hands. This reaction is used by forensic scientists to reveal a criminal's fingerprints.

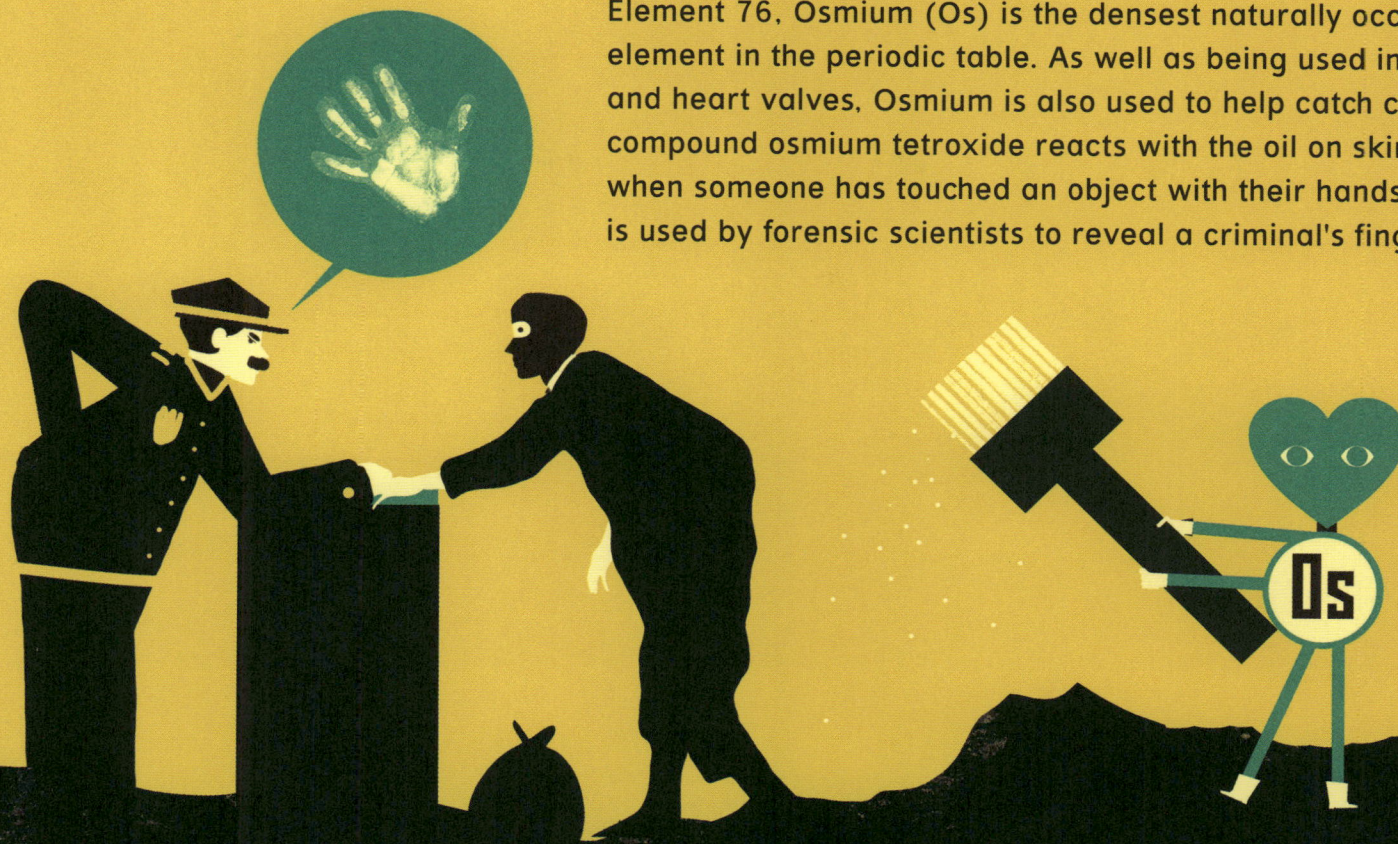

The density of an object or substance is calculated by dividing its mass by its volume. The more dense an object or substance is, the heavier it feels for its size.

The most interesting story behind the name of a transition metal belongs to cobalt (Co). It comes from the German word 'kobold', which refers to a type of goblin. Medieval miners believed that child-sized imps were to blame for wreaking havoc. What they thought was silver ore actually produced worthless lumps of a silvery-blue metal and toxic gases that made them fall ill.

An unlikely place to find cobalt is in the stomach of a cow. Bacteria there use cobalt ions to transform molecules into vitamin B12. This vitamin helps to keep the cow's nerve and blood cells healthy.

Post-Transition Metals

To the right of the transition metals you will find a group known as the **POST-TRANSITION METALS**. They go by other names, too, including 'poor metals'. **They are softer than the transition metals, and often have lower melting and boiling points.** Gallium (Ga) for example, would melt in your hand.

Lead (Pb) is by far the most famous of the post-transition metals, and is used in many different ways. In the 1500s, the English monarch Queen Elizabeth I famously used a face whitener made of lead mixed with vinegar and water. Unfortunately, nobody knew at the time that lead is poisonous, and it is thought to have contributed to her death in 1603.

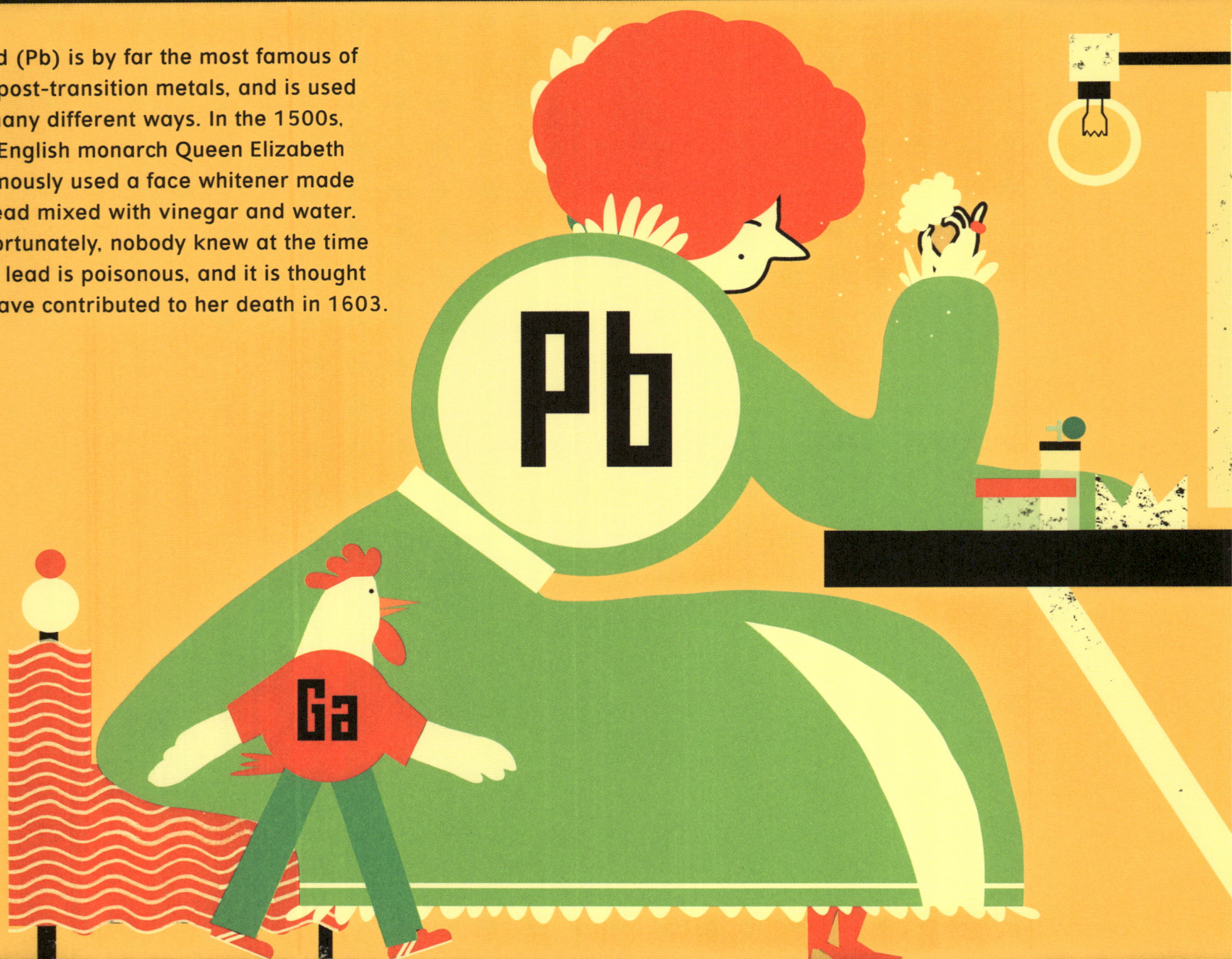

Lead also used to be added to petrol to reduce engine noise before its dangers were fully known. That's why you'll often see petrol today labelled as 'unleaded'.

The element thallium (Ti) is also toxic, and the compound thallium sulfate was commonly used in rat poison and insecticides for most of the 1900s. Thallium sulfate is both odourless and tasteless, so it is hard to know if you've accidentally been exposed to it. Since the 1970s, Thallium sulfate is no longer used because of the risk of accidental poisoning.

Makeup made of lead may now be considered a bad idea, but another (non-toxic) post-transition metal is still used as a pigment today. The silvery, pink-tinged metal bismuth (Bi) is found in eye shadow, hair sprays and nail polishes, adding a pearly shimmer. Bismuth has a similar density to lead, so is often a good replacement for its more toxic fellow post-transition metal.

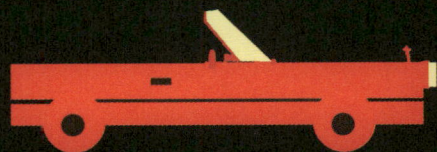

Reactive Non-Metals

Tucked away in the top right-hand side of the periodic table is a small but very important set of elements: THE NON-METALS. **They are made up of three groups: noble gases, halogens and reactive non-metals.** Here we'll focus on the last of those, the reactive non-metals – a varied group that make up almost all of you.

The reactive non-metals are the ingredients for all life on Earth. From butterflies to buffalo, bacteria to birds, living things are built using carbon (C), hydrogen (H) – the only non-metal not found in this area) – nitrogen (N), oxygen (O), phosphorus (P) and sulphur (S).

The bright-yellow element sulphur has been known about since ancient times and was regarded by ALCHEMISTS, **scientists from the Middle Ages who tried to turn chemicals into gold**, as one of three substances that make up everything in the Universe.

Many compounds of sulphur have a very unpleasant smell and are responsible for the strong odours of rotten eggs, garlic and skunks.

Sulphuric acid is widely used in making fertiliser, as well as in the fungicides and pesticides used to protect fruit and vegetables.

However, during World War I, sulphur created devastating damage, when it was used as a chemical weapon called 'mustard gas'.

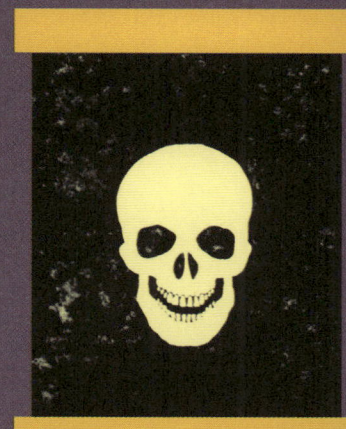

Phosphorus was discovered in a very unusual way. In the 1660s, German chemist **HENNIG BRAND** left 50 buckets of urine alone for many days until they started to smell extremely bad. He then boiled the disgusting liquid and passed the evaporated gas through water until he was left with a thick paste. That led him to discover a new substance that glowed in the dark: phosphorus. It was one of the earliest non-metals to be identified.

Phosphorus can catch alight easily in air and was used in the heads of matches in the 1800s. Many matchstick factory workers were exposed to dangerous levels of the element.

Metalloids

For thousands of years some elements have been used for sinister purposes. If you're an evil villain looking for a poison, you turn to a group of elements called the METALLOIDS. **They behave partly like metals and partly like non-metals.** They often look like metals, but they are brittle and not good at conducting electricity.

Arsenic (As) has been known as the 'King of Poisons' since the days of the Roman Empire. It is very toxic to humans. An antidote was developed in the 1800s by ROBERT BUNSEN (see page 28). This was particularly fortunate, because an explosion in his laboratory years later left him with arsenic poisoning. His life was saved by the antidote he had invented!

The colour green came into fashion in Victorian Britain thanks to the attractive dye arsenic produces. People rushed to buy green clothing, green curtains and green wallpaper – unaware they could become victims of arsenic poisoning.

Some chemists disagree about which elements should be included in this small group of metalloid elements., but the six usual members are silicon (Si), boron (B), germanium (Ge), arsenic, antimony (Sb) and tellurium (Te).

As carbon's (C) next-door neighbour in the periodic table, boron shares the same properties of toughness and heat resistance. Boron is mostly used in the production of glass and ceramics, although you'll also find it in golf clubs, fishing rods and bulletproof vests.

Boron is a crucial ingredient for plant growth, too. It helps them transport sugar and grow good seeds and pollen. Although too much boron can be poisonous to other living things, including insects.

Our use of antimony dates back thousands of years. The ancient Egyptians used it as a rich, black eye makeup, the ancient Greeks used it to treat skin infections and in the Middle Ages it was used as a medicinal laxative.

Some people believe antimony takes its name from the Greek *anti-monachos*, which means 'monk-killer'. This could be true, as many early chemists were also monks and, like arsenic, antimony can be deadly.

R.I.P.

Halogens

There is a small group of five non-metals that often combine with metals to make salts. Chemists call them HALOGENS, from the Greek words *hal* (salt) and *gen* (to produce). You'll find them in Group 17 – the second-to-last column of the periodic table.

Chlorine (Cl) is one of the best-known halogens. It combines with the alkali metal sodium to make sodium chloride – otherwise known as the table salt you put on your fish and chips. On its own, chlorine is a yellowy-green toxic gas. Today, you are more likely to find chlorine in a swimming pool or drinking water as hypochlorous acid, which is used to kill bacteria.

Inside Your Stomach:

Chlorine is inside you, too! Hydrochloric acid in your stomach helps with the job of breaking down the food you eat.

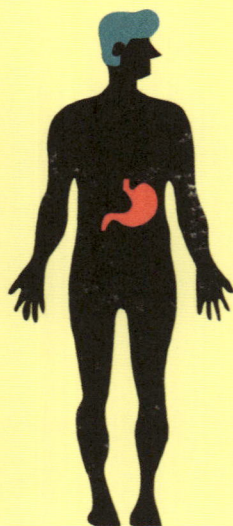

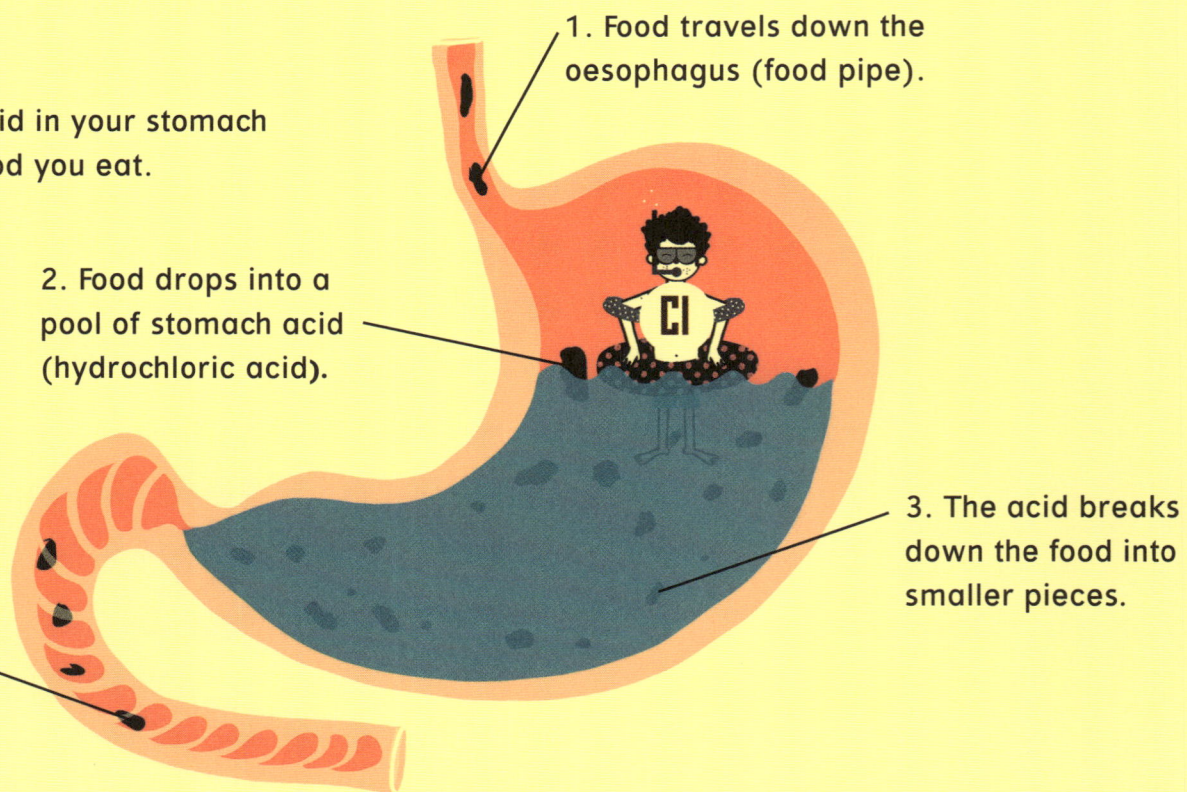

1. Food travels down the oesophagus (food pipe).

2. Food drops into a pool of stomach acid (hydrochloric acid).

3. The acid breaks down the food into smaller pieces.

4. Once ready, food travels into your intestine.

Bromine (Br) is a very unusual element. It is the only non-metal that is liquid at normal room temperature – its melting point is -7 degrees Celsius. The metal mercury (Hg) is the only other element that shares this property. Bromine containing molecules is often used as fire retardant.

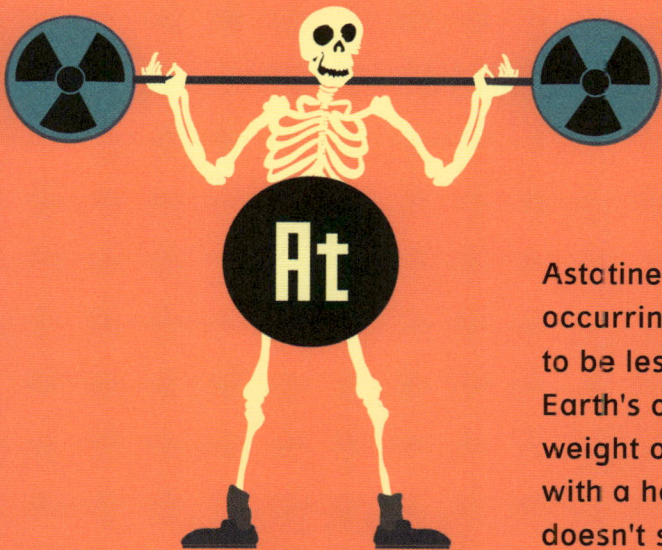

08:00

Astatine (At) is the rarest naturally occurring element. There is thought to be less than a gram present in the Earth's crust at any one time – about the weight of a paperclip. It is radioactive, with a half-life of around 8 hours, so it doesn't stick around for long!

In 1811 French chemist BERNARD COURTOIS discovered the purple-black element iodine (I) in seaweed ash. Iodine is fairly rare, but it is an essential nutrient in the human diet. Seawater is a good source of iodine, and therefore so are seaweed and fish. It can also be found in eggs and milk. Too little iodine can stop your thyroid gland from working properly, and the thyroid gland is important as it keeps every cell in your body working. Iodine has many uses, including in disinfectants, dyes and photography chemicals.

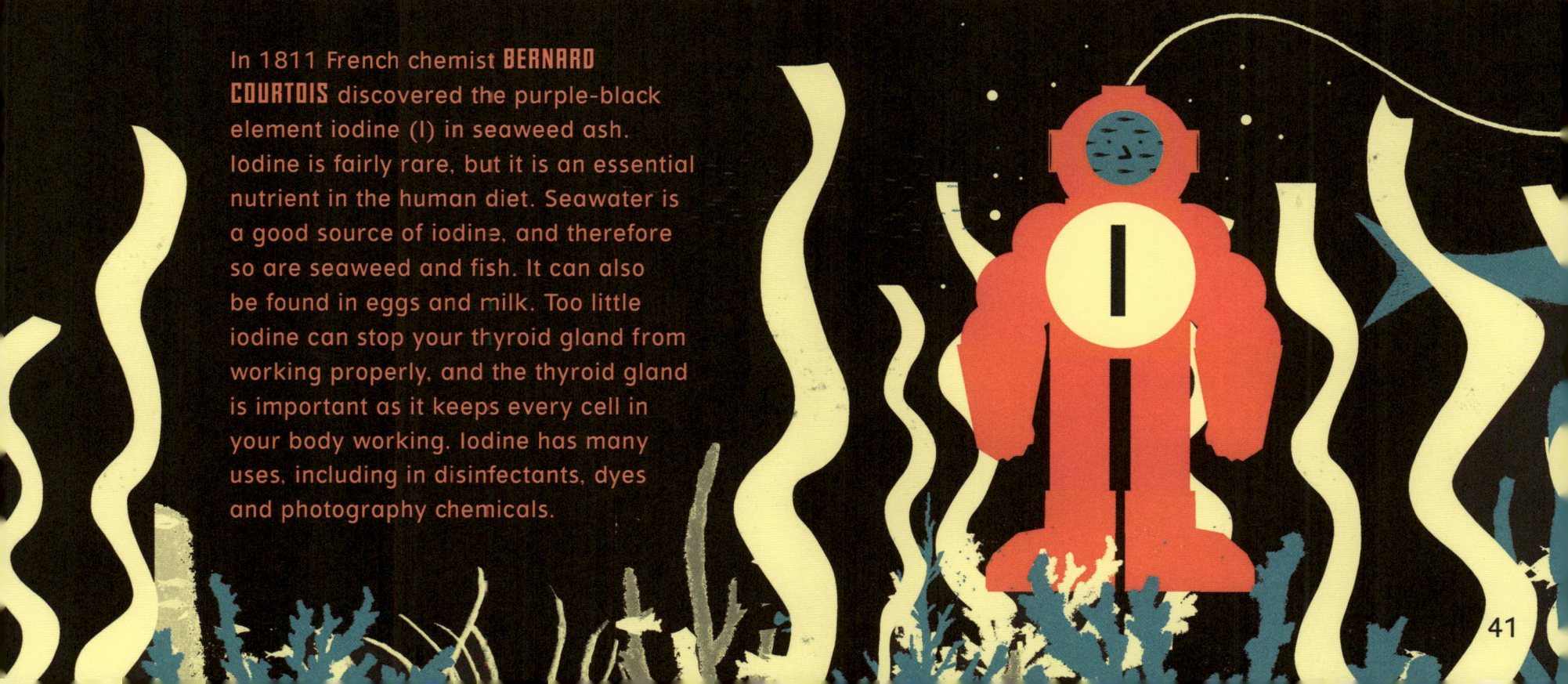

The Noble Gases

There are some elements that are perfectly happy by themselves. The **NOBLE GASES tend to have no smell, no colour and generally don't get involved in reactions with other elements**. However, they all glow brightly when electricity is passed through them. They occupy the final column of the periodic table.

Other than helium (He) – which is used in floating birthday balloons – the noble gas you're most likely to have heard of is neon (Ne). It glows reddish-orange when electricity is passed through it and that's why it has often been used in colourful, eye-catching advertising signs. 'Neon' signs actually contain a mixture of several different noble gases.

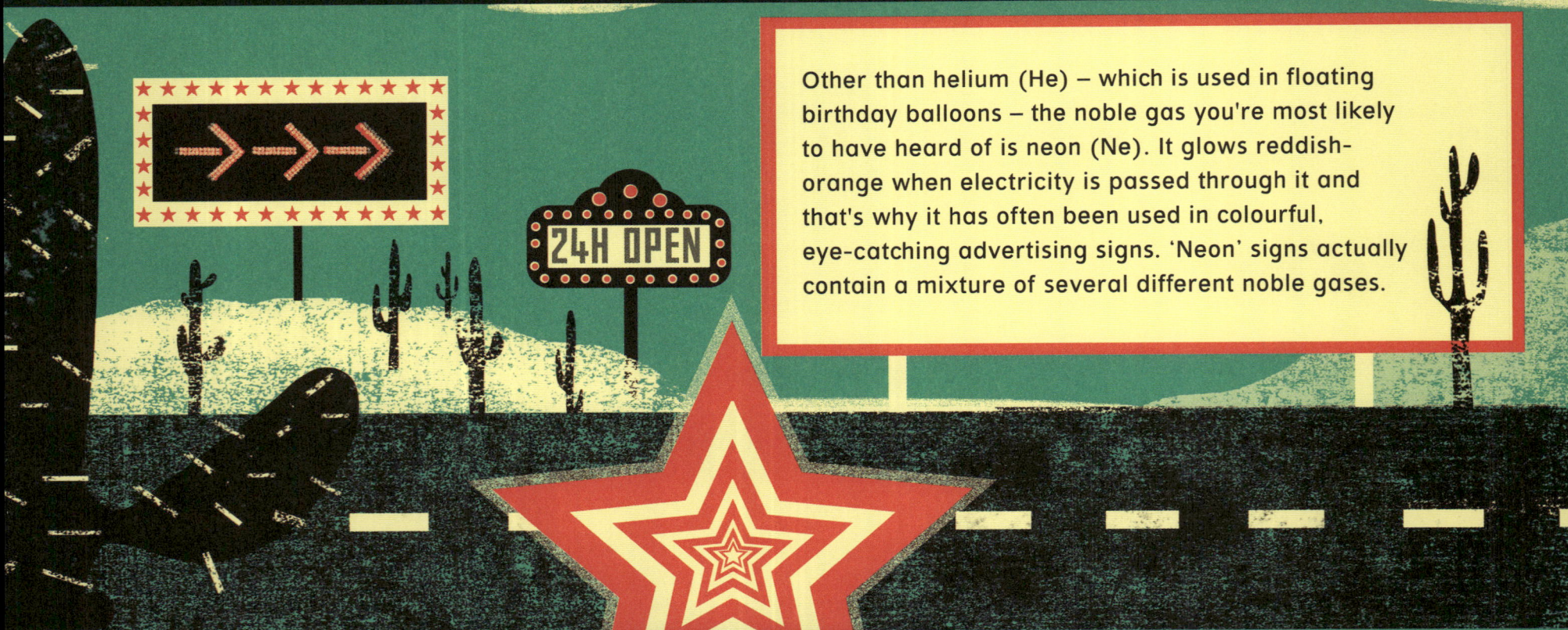

24H OPEN

The most abundant noble gas in the air we breathe is argon (Ar). It makes up just under one per cent of Earth's atmosphere. There is more argon in the air than water vapour. That's partly why argon was the first noble gas to be discovered by Ramsay, four years before he discovered neon, krypton (Kr) and xenon (Xe). If you are reading this book under an incandescent light, thank argon – it's the gas inside the bulb.

Ar

Chemists **WILLIAM RAMSAY** and **MORRIS TRAVERS** discovered krypton and xenon, which had secretly been in the air all along. They named krypton after an ancient Greek word meaning 'the hidden one' and xenon means 'stranger'. Xenon is now used in extremely powerful space rocket engines.

Krypton shares a similar name to the fictional material kryptonite, Superman's one weakness.

Neon was first discovered in 1898 in London, also by Ramsay and Travers, who turned a sample of air to liquid and investigated its contents.

The highly radioactive gas radon (Rn) is produced as other elements found in rock and soil undergo radioactive decay. While this gas can be dangerous to living things, some people think it has helped species evolve over many generations, as the radiation causes changes to their DNA.

43

The Lanthanides

Look closely and you'll notice that there is a break in the periodic table. Arrows mark the place where the atomic numbers stop going up by one. Two rows have been moved to sit beneath the rest: the lanthanides and the actinides. This is a clever trick to make sure the table can easily fit on one page. It's a bit like storing stuff in a basement to save space.

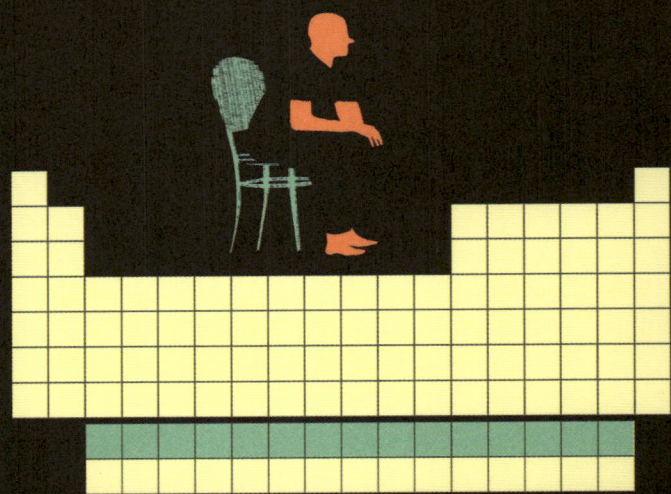

The LANTHANIDES are reactive, silvery-coloured metals. They get their name from the first member of this group – lanthanum (La), and all 15 members share similar properties. Only one element in the group, promethium (Pm), doesn't occur naturally on Earth.

Along with lanthanum, you'll find praseodymium (Pr) on a TV or film set – both elements are used extensively in studio lighting.

DIRECTOR La

Pr

Lanthanum is useful for clearing unwanted algae from outdoor swimming pools. It removes the food that the tiny plants feed on and that stops the water from turning green. Lanthanum is also essential for a type of bacteria that lives in volcanic mud pools. It helps them absorb the methane they need to survive.

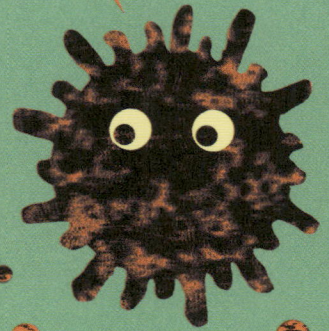

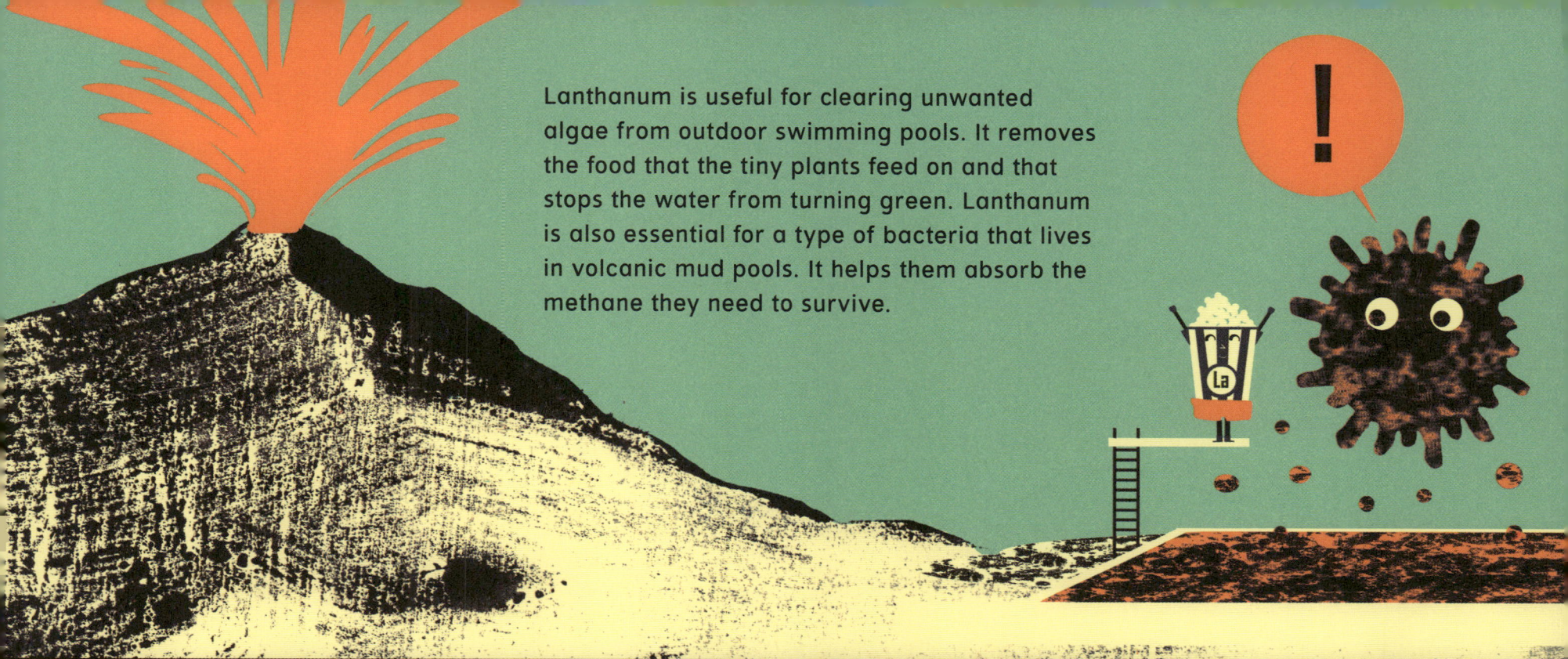

!

Praseodymium stains glass and ceramics a vivid yellowy colour, called 'praseodymium yellow'. When mixed with neodymium (Nd) it becomes a material known as didymium, which is used in the goggles that welders wear. Didymium protects their eyes from bright flashes by blocking out the yellow light.

Nd

NORMAL GLASS

DIDYMIUM GLASS

The rarest of the lanthanides is thulium (Tm). It is named after Thule, the ancient name of a region close to modern-day Scandinavia, home of the Vikings. Tiny amounts are added to Euro banknotes. The thulium glows when you shine ultraviolet light on it, making it easier to tell if the notes are fake.

BCE ECB EZB EKT EKP 2002

Tm

5

5 EURO

The Actinides

Like the lanthanides, the **ACTINIDES** get their name from the first element in the group – actinium (Ac). **All fifteen of the elements in this group are radioactive.** That's why they are mostly used in nuclear weapons and nuclear power stations.

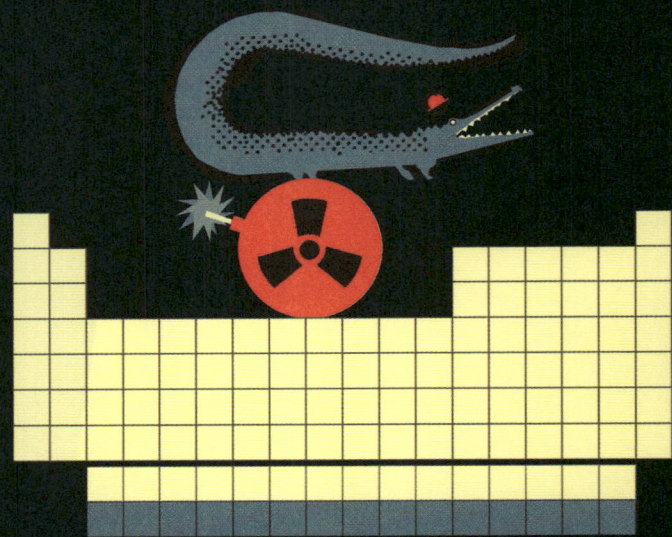

Due to its radioactivity, actinium glows in the dark with a blueish light, as the radiation it produces excites the surrounding air to glow, like in a fluorescent light bulb. Its radioactivity also means it is a good source of particles called neutrons (see page 10), which are used to scan baggage at airports to check for banned items.

The very rare element protactinium (Pa) is only obtained from uranium ore in tiny amounts. Oceanographers track the movement of sediments on the sea floor by measuring levels of naturally produced protactinium at the bottom of the ocean. It allows them to work out how the flow of water in the world's oceans changed after the glaciers melted at the end of the last Ice Age.

Some of the actinides have only ever been created by humans inside laboratories. Berkelium (Bk) is named after the Lawrence Berkeley National Laboratory in California, USA, where it was discovered in 1949. Only a single gram of berkelium has ever been produced – about the same weight as a small paperclip. Aside from its association with scientific research, Berkeley has a long history of protests, including for peace during the Vietnam War.

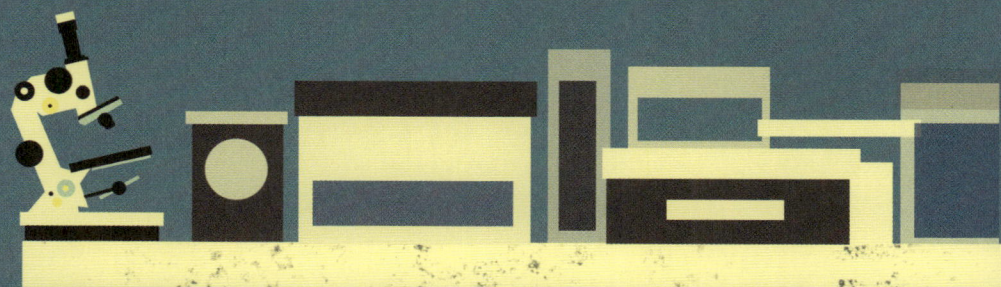

Californium (Cf) was also discovered at Berkeley and takes its name from the US state where the lab is based. If it is absorbed by the human body then it can affect its ability to produce red blood cells, so Californium needs to be handled very carefully.

Nobel Prize Winners

There is one award that every scientist wants to win – the Nobel Prize. It is named after the Swedish chemist and entrepreneur **ALFRED NOBEL** who invented dynamite. The element nobelium (No) is named in his honour. Nobel used his vast fortune to set up the awards to recognise leading figures in physics, chemistry, medicine, literature and peace. Winners receive a special gold medal and around $1 million.

A super select band of scientists have 'done the double' – winning a Nobel Prize and having an element named after them. The first ever Nobel Prize for Physics was awarded in 1901 to German physicist **WILHELM RÖNTGEN**, who had discovered X-rays in 1895. The first-ever X-ray photograph shows the bones in his wife's hand. The superheavy element roentgenium (Rg) is extremely radioactive and was first made inside a laboratory in 1994. Ten years later it was named in Röntgen's honour.

The most famous recipient of both honours is **ALBERT EINSTEIN** – he gives his name to the ninety-ninth element einsteinium (Es) and he won the 1921 physics prize. Einsteinium was discovered during the first explosion of a hydrogen bomb in 1952.

Danish physicist **NIELS BOHR** won the physics prize the year after Einstein and he is honoured in the periodic table with bohrium (Bh). Bohr was the first to realise that the electrons inside atoms can only exist in certain orbits.

The first person to split the atom was New Zealand physicist **ERNEST RUTHERFORD**. He won the 1908 Nobel Prize for Chemistry. Rutherfordium (Rf) was almost called kurchatovium after Soviet nuclear physicist Igor Kurchatov, because the element was jointly discovered in Russia.

Fermium (Fm) is named after the Italian physicist **ENRICO FERMI** (Physics, 1938) and lawrencium (Lr) after American nuclear scientist **ERNEST LAWRENCE** (Physics, 1939). However, only one Nobel Prize winner has had an element named after them in their lifetime: American chemist **GLENN T. SEABORG**. He won the chemistry prize in 1951 for discovering ten elements, including element 106, Seaborgium (Sg).

Pioneering Women

Of the 118 elements currently featured in the periodic table, only 15 are named after the scientists who discovered them. Only two elements are named after women. Yet many more female scientists played a significant part behind the scenes. Sadly often without the credit their hard work deserved.

The story of Polish chemist and physicist **MARIE CURIE** is both inspirational and tragic. She was the first woman to win a Nobel Prize (Physics, 1903). She also won the chemistry prize in 1911 and remains the only woman to have won two Nobel prizes.

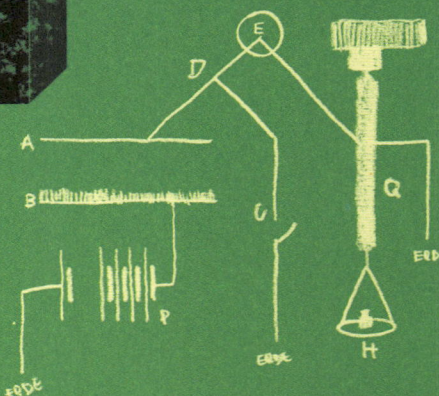

Curie discovered two new elements – polonium (Po) and radium (Ra) – and pioneered the theory of 'radioactivity', a word that she coined. She died in 1934 having become ill after exposure to the radioactive elements she regularly worked with. Her husband Pierre – also a scientist and Nobel Prize winner – died in 1906 when he was run over by a horse-drawn cart in a Parisian street where they lived.

The radioactive element curium (Cm), discovered in 1944 by a team led by Glenn Seaborg, is named after both the Curies.

In 1925, the German chemist **IDA NODDACK** discovered the element rhenium (Re) alongside her husband, Walter. It took several attempts to find what was sometimes known as the invisble element. She was nominated for the Nobel Prize in Chemistry three times, but never won. Noddack was also the first person to suggest the idea of nuclear fission. Her theory was ignored at the time, but just five years later, Otto Hahn went on to win the Nobel Prize for demonstrating fission. Thankfully, today Noddack is better recognised for her contributions.

The only other woman to have an element named after her is Austrian physicist **LISE MEITNER**. A keen scientist from a young age, Meitner used to keep a notebook of her experiments underneath her pillow. She played a key role in discovering the way uranium breaks apart, a crucial part of harnessing nuclear energy. She also co-discovered the element protactinium (Pa).

Meitner was similarly overlooked by the Nobel Prize committee, but the element meitnerium (Mt) was named after her in 1992.

Commendable Men

Other than Mendeelev, there are four male scientists who have elements named after them, but haven't won a Nobel Prize. Three of them lived and worked before the first prizes were awarded in 1901. One is a transition metal (see pages 32–33), and two belong to the lanthanides (see pages 44–45). One, Oganesson, is in group 8, likely a noble element, but not a gas.

The first person to have an element named for them was VASILI SAMARSKY-BYKHOVETS, a Russian soldier and mining engineer. He slots into the table in the form of samarium (Sm) – a hard, silvery metal. This element is used to make powerful magnets, which were used in *Solar Challenger*, the first solar-powered plane capable of long distance flights. It is also found in headphones.

The Finnish scientist JOHAN GADOLIN (1760–1852) lends his name to gadolinium (Gd), a soft reactive metal, which was discovered 28 years after his death. Gadolin was a man of many talents – he spoke a whopping seven languages and was knighted three times for his achievements in science. Gadolin is also known for writing a description of the first rare-earth element, yttrium (Y).

The most well-known of the quartet is Polish mathematician **NICOLAUS COPERNICUS** (1473–1543). Copernicus is remembered for **correctly suggesting that the Earth orbits the Sun, rather than the other way around.** A tiny amount of the element copernicium (Cn) was first created in a laboratory in Germany in 1996, and named to honour Copernicus's contribution to science.

YURI OGANESSIAN is the only person, other than Glenn Seaborg, to have an element named after them while they were still alive. The Russian **nuclear physicist is the head of the Joint Institute for Nuclear Research, near Moscow**. His international team of scientists have been involved in the discovery of every element between 107 and 118. That last element was named oganesson (Og) in 2016. It is exceedingly rare – only a handful of oganesson atoms have ever been created.

Myths and Legends

Throughout human history we have told each other amazing stories and filled the pages of countless books with sorcerers and kings, mysterious creatures and fantastic beasts. It's no surprise that scientists have often turned to these myths and legends for inspiration when naming new elements.

Thorium (Th) is named after Thor, the Norse god of thunder and lightning famous for his powerful hammer. The element itself is radioactive, but it decays incredibly slowly with a half-life that's roughly the same as the age of the Universe.

Have you ever heard someone describe something as tantalising? We get that word from the Greek mythological king called Tantalus who stole food from the gods. His punishment was to stand under a tree for eternity surrounded by low-hanging fruit that were forever just out of his reach. The rare silvery metal tantalum (Ta) is named after him. It is an excellent conductor of electricity and is used to make video games consoles and computers. Almost always found with tantalum is the element niobium (Nb), named after Tantalus's daughter, Niobe, the Greek goddess of tears.

Other elements named after myths and legends include mercury (Hg), which is named after the messenger of the gods in Roman mythology. Sometimes called 'quicksilver', it is one of only two elements that are liquid at room temperature, which is one of the reasons why it is ideal for use in thermometers. Iridium (Ir) – a super-dense and corrosion-resistant metal – is named after Iris, the Greek goddess of the rainbow, because it makes salts with bright colours. It is also used in compass bearings.

Prometheus was also a thief – he stole fire from the Greek gods. His punishment was to have his liver pecked out by an eagle. Each night it would regrow and each day the bird would return to do it all over again. Promethium (Pm) isn't found in measurable amounts in Earth's crust, but traces can be found in uranium ores. Scientists have come up with clever ways to make it from uranium (U) and neodymium (Nd).

The Solar System

During the 1700s and 1800s, astronomers discovered lots of new and amazing objects scattered throughout the solar system, including the planets Uranus and Neptune. More than half of the elements were also discovered during this time, with scientists drawing on the astronomical discoveries for inspiration when naming new elements.

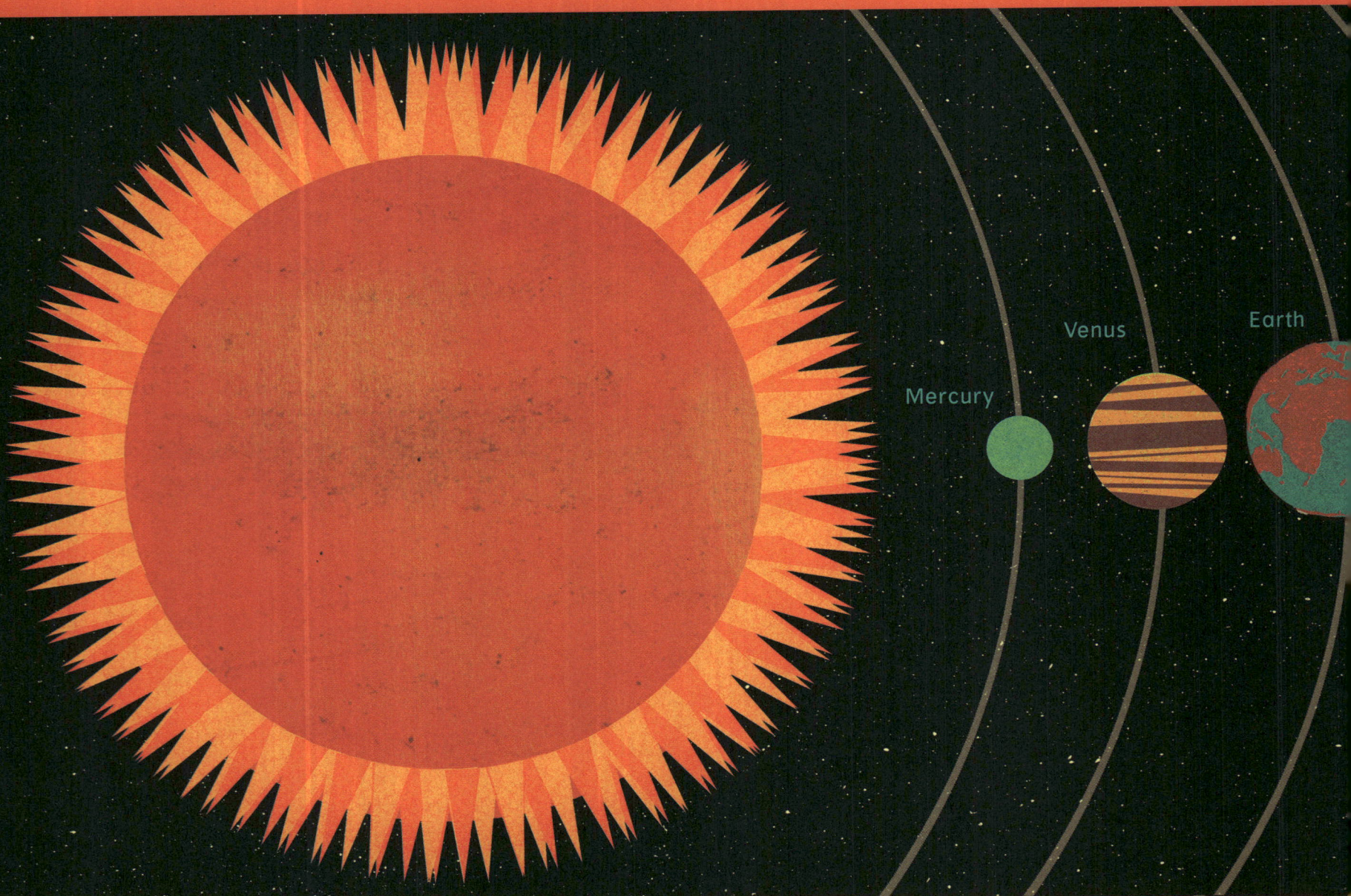

Mercury

Venus

Earth

The element helium (He) was discovered in the Sun by astronomers before it was identified by chemists on Earth (see pages 18-19). That's where its name comes from – *helios* is the Greek word for the Sun. Likewise, selenium (Se) – used to give a red colour to glass and found naturally in a skunk's foul-smelling spray – is named after the Greek word for the Moon, *Selene*. Selenium's properties are similar to tellurium (Te), which took its name from *tellus* – the Latin word for Earth. Ironically, it is one of the rarest elements on our planet, but is abundant in space.

Two asteroids are also commemorated in the periodic table. Cerium (Ce) – a soft, silvery-white metal – is named after dwarf planet and the largest body in the asteroid belt found between Mars and Jupiter. Ceres. Cerium makes sparks and burns when heated, making it ideal for use in lighters. Palladium (Pd) – used in jewellery and dentistry – takes its name from Pallas, the second biggest asteroid.

asteroid belt

Mars

Jupiter

Saturn

Uranus

Neptune

German chemist **MARTIN HEINRICH KLAPROTH** first identified the radioactive metal uranium (U) in 1789, naming it after the planet Uranus that had been discovered just eight years earlier. Today, we use uranium to generate energy in nuclear power plants.

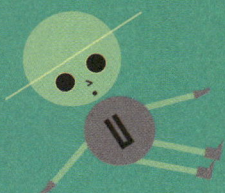

Uranium has the atomic number 92, so when a new element with atomic number 93 was found in 1940 it was named neptunium (Np) as Neptune is the next planet after Uranus. The discovery of plutonium (Pu) – atomic number 94 – was announced the following year.

Continents and Countries

When you stare at the periodic table you might be surprised to know there is a map of the world hiding within the elements. Take a close look at this world map and see how many you can identify.

Two elements - americum (Am) and europium (Eu) – are named after continents. Europium is so reactive that it has to be stored under water to shelter it from the oxygen in the air.

Two elements name-check France – francium (Fr) and gallium (Ga). The latter is named after Gaul – an old name for the region that contained modern France. Francium is extremely radioactive and contains a half-life of just 22 minutes.

Americium is used in smoke detectors.

Gallium has the highest boiling point of any element, so it's used to make high-temperature thermometers.

Six elements take their name from countries. Polonium (Po) is named after Poland and Germanium after Germany. Polonium was used to power early Mars rovers. It is also a poison.

Russia gets its own element too – ruthenium (Ru) comes from *Ruthenia*, the Latin name for the country. It was discovered by Russian scientist KARL ERNST CLAUS in 1844. The nibs of fountain pens are often coated with a material partly made of ruthenium.

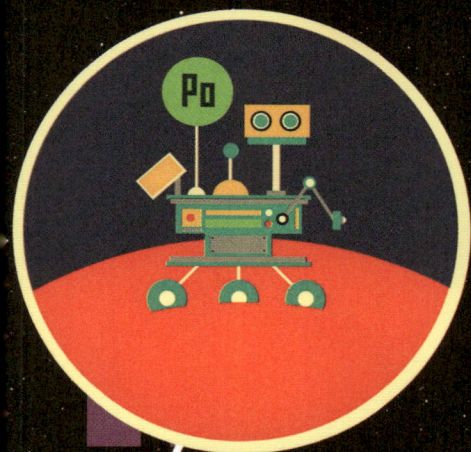

You'll find germanium (Ge) in camera lenses, guitar pedals and some TVs. Some of your favourite music might have sounded totally different if it wasn't for the germanium in guitar pedals that give them a smooth, soft tone.

Super-heavy element Nihonium (Nh) honours Japan. Nihon is a Japenese term for Japan. Like francium, this element is extremely radioactive, but disappears even faster – it has a half-life of just 20 seconds!

Capital Cities

Tens of millions of tourists descend on these famous cities every year to gaze at their world famous landmarks. But Paris, Copenhagen, Moscow and Stockholm are also hidden away in the periodic table. Element 115 moscovium (Mc) is the most obvious, but some of the others take a little detective work.

Chemist **PER TEODOR CLEVE** named holmium (Ho) after the Swedish capital, Stockholm, where he was born. Holmium has the highest magnetic strength of any element, so you'll find it used in magnets. Researchers are still trying to work out how we can utilise this property to our advantage, but they think it may be possible to use it in quantum computers in the future.

Of these four elements, moscovium is by far the rarest. It doesn't occur naturally and was first made in 2003 at the Joint Institute for Nuclear Research in Russia. Just a handful of atoms of this super-heavy element have ever been created and, with a half-life of just 220 milliseconds, blink and you'll miss it!

The rare metal lutetium (Lu) takes its name from the Roman city of Lutetia, which later became Paris – the native city of one of the scientists who discovered it **GEORGES URBAIN**, and home of the Mona Lisa. In 53 BCE, Julius Caesar used Lutetia as the location to gather all the Gallic tribes together to discuss politics and war. Oil refineries use lutetium to break down long chains of carbon atoms to help turn them into petrol and natural gas.

Transition metal hafnium (Hf) was discovered in Copenhagen in 1923 and was named after *Hafnia* – the Latin name for the Danish capital. It was one of the missing elements originally predicted by Dmitri Mendeleev in 1869. Hafnium also has an out-of-this-world history. It is resistant to corrosion and extreme temperatures, and was used by NASA in the nozzle of the Apollo Lunar Lander that helped the first astronauts blast off the Moon and return to the Earth in 1969.

Ytterby

The coast of Sweden near its capital Stockholm is dotted all around with 30,000 tiny islands. Among them is Resarö, home to just 3,000 people. You would almost never know that one of its little villages made huge contributions to the periodic table, but Ytterby appears more times in the periodic table than any other place on the planet.

In 1787, a Swedish army officer called CARL AXEL ARRHENIUS visited a mine and stumbled across a heavy black stone that seemed out of place. Arrhenius sent the rock to his scientist friends, hoping they'd tell him it was a new source of the metal tungsten. Surprisingly, the rock contained a new, unidentified element. It was named yttrium (Y). Over the next century and a bit, a staggering eight further elements were found in the Ytterby mine. Three are also named after the village: terbium (Tb), erbium (Er) and ytterbium (Yb). Today the mine is a protected monument in recognition of its important history.

In the first colour television sets, yttrium was important in displaying the colour red. Similarly, when combined with oxygen (O), erbium can be used to give objects like sunglasses a pink tinge.

Have you ever noticed that a clock at home eventually stops telling the time accurately and you have to correct it? In special timekeepers called atomic clocks, a thousand ytterbium atoms are trapped in a grid made of laser beams. Atomic clocks can run for longer than the age of the Universe (13.8 billion years) before they get a second out of step because the yttrium gives them some of the most accurate ticks in the world.

Yb

Ship builders use terbium as part of the sonar system on boats and submarines, which helps them check their distance from the sea floor.

Tb

In the Home

You don't have to visit a chemistry lab to get up close with the periodic table. There is a whole host of familiar and unusual elements right under your nose in your own home, whether you're in the bedroom, bathroom, kitchen or living room.

We spend roughly a third of our lives – up to 200,000 hours over our lifetime – asleep. All the more reason to make sure you have a comfortable mattress! Hiding inside it is an element helping you sleep soundly. Mattresses get their bounce from a series of metal springs and these are often made of steel coated with the element vanadium (V). It makes the springs stronger and stops them from rusting. These properties make vanadium perfect for jet engines, too.

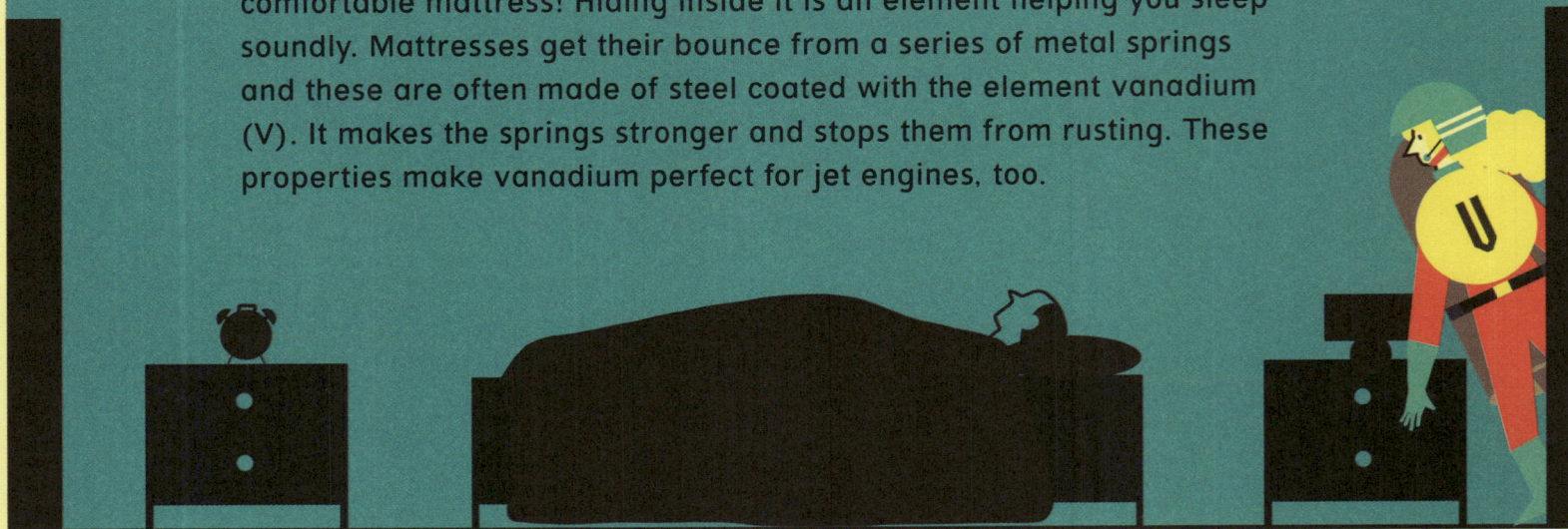

Turn on the taps to run a bubble bath and hot water fills your tub. A network of pipes made of the element copper (Cu) probably carried the water around your house. This reddish-gold, lightweight metal is easy for plumbers to bend into shape and it doesn't corrode easily, so the pipes last a long time. You'll find copper in electrical equipment, such as wiring, too, because it is very good at conducting heat and electricity.

You should always brush your teeth before heading to bed. But have you ever wondered what's actually in your toothpaste? It contains fluoride, a compound of the element fluorine (F), to help prevent tooth decay. Sometimes fluorides are also added to tap water for the same reason.

You might find the element chromium (Cr) in the kitchen drawer. A lot of cutlery is made from stainless steel, which contains about ten per cent chromium to help prevent corrosion. Chromium gets it name from *chroma*, the Greek word for colour, because it produces the many beautiful colours seen in gemstones.

Technology

Since the start of the twenty-first century the number of gadgets and gizmos we use in our everyday lives has exploded. Now it is hard to imagine the world without technology. Yet many of the appliances we use today wouldn't work without some of the more obscure elements in the periodic table.

Smartphones, for example, contain dozens of different elements.

The touchscreen works by conducting electricity across a thin film on its surface. The film is made from a mixture of indium oxide and tin oxide. Indium (In) is the softest non-alkali metal – you can easily scratch it with your fingernail. It also has one of the lowest melting points of any metal and makes a high-pitched squeak when bent.

Neodymium (Nd) is used to make some of the most powerful magnets in the world, and magnets are what make headphones, speakers and microphones work. Even a tiny neodymium magnet can still pack a punch, perfect for modern slim devices.

Lithium-ion batteries are the small but mighty sources of energy that keep our hand-held technology charged up and us connected with the world. The invention of these rechargeable power stores has totally changed the way we use technology.

Phones often vibrate when they receive a text message or call. Dysprosium (Dy) is used to make the motor responsible for the vibration. Only about 100 tonnes of dysprosium are produced worldwide each year, mostly in China. If you shared it out equally among every human on Earth, each of us would get just 0.01 grams – about the same weight as a house fly.

The Human Body

You have a personal relationship with the elements of the periodic table – some of them are helping to keep you alive. In fact, a total of 60 different elements go into making you!

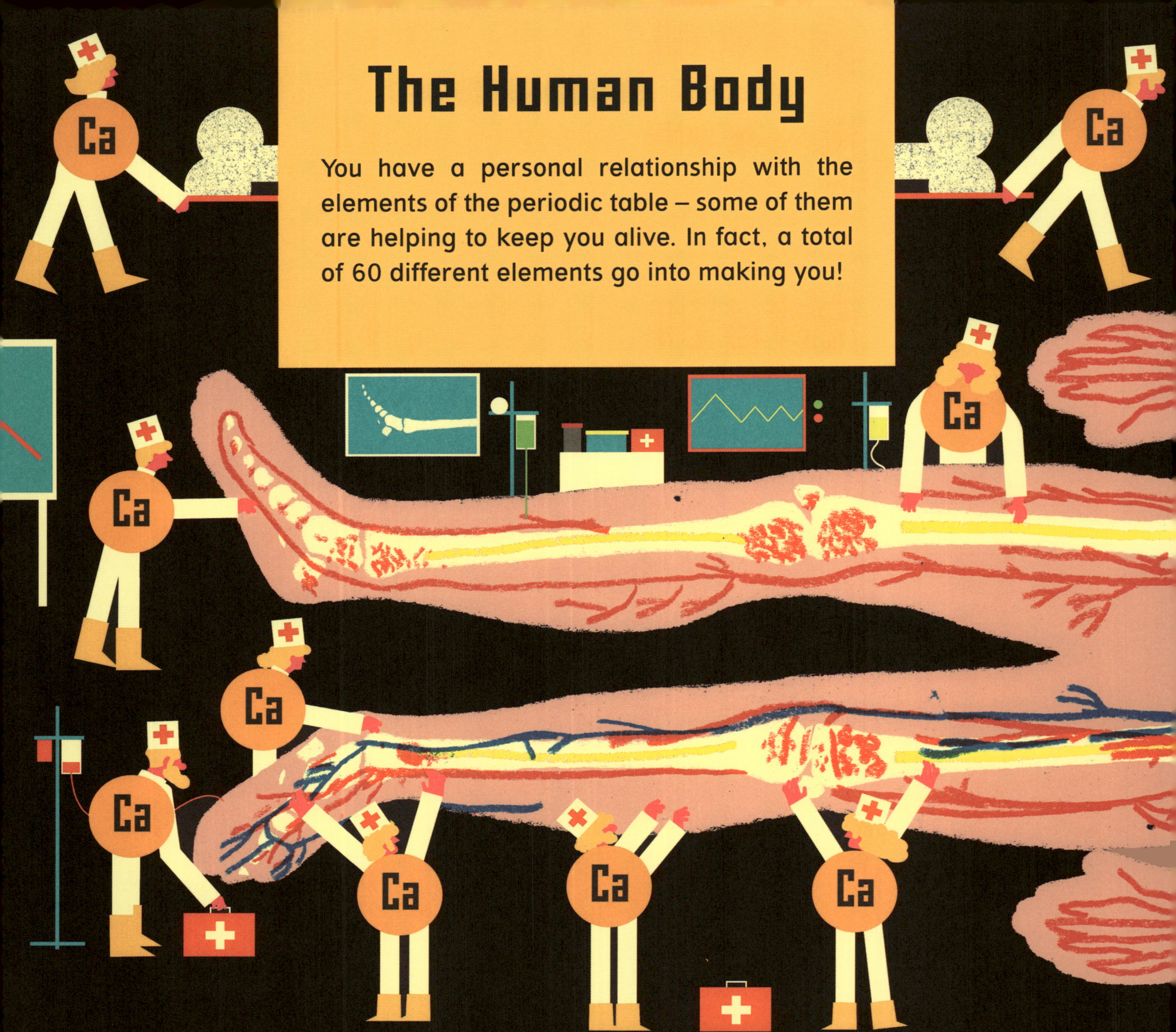

Over your lifetime you will breathe in over 200 million litres of air. Hidden inside the gas are molecules of oxygen (O) that your cells need to make energy. But how does it get from your lungs to those cells? Special couriers called red blood cells deliver it there as your heart pumps blood around your body. Red blood cells contain a chemical called haemoglobin, which in turn contains the element iron (Fe). The iron binds to the oxygen so that it can be transported around your body. The average adult body contains about four grams of iron – about the weight of eight raisins.

The human body contains about a kilogram of calcium (Ca) – mostly inside bones. If you break your leg, your body will build new bone by placing calcium and phosphorus (P) into a crystal structure on top of a scaffold made of chemicals called proteins. Calcium also helps your heart keep a regular rhythm and your blood clot if you cut yourself.

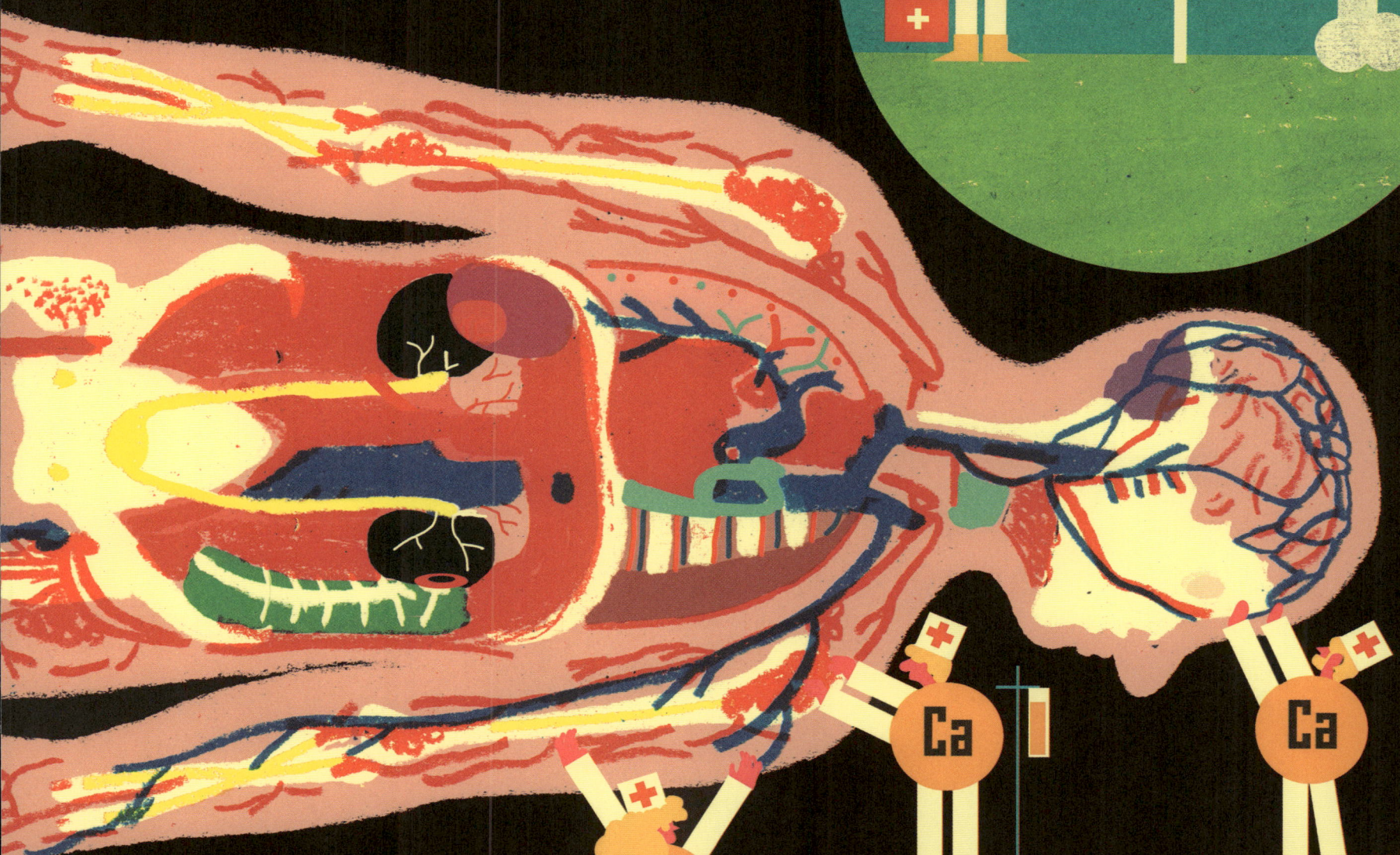

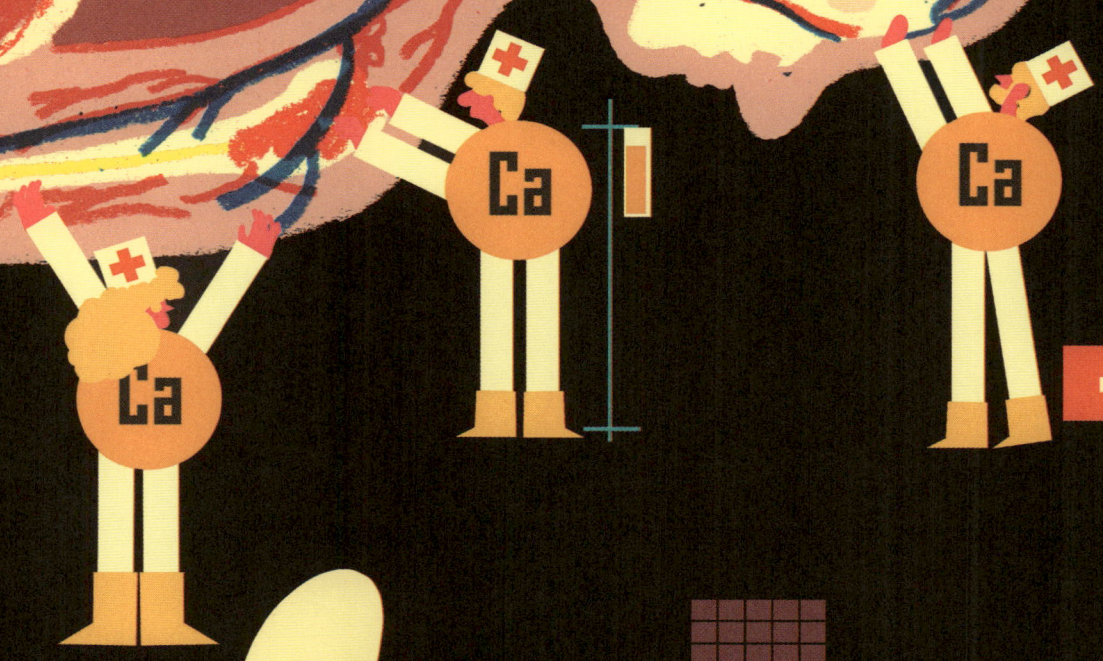

Ca + P =

It is important that you get enough potassium (K) in your diet. Potassium is crucial for good brain function and memory. Bananas, avocados, nuts and dark chocolate are all great sources of it.

Fizzing Fireworks

Every year, cities around the world compete to put on the most spectacular New Year's fireworks display. Millions are spent on illuminating the sky with colourful explosions for just a few minutes. But have you ever stopped to wonder what goes into a firework? The answer is normally salt – just not the kind you put on your food. It is packed into pea-sized pellets called stars, which burst into showers of colour.

The story goes that fireworks were invented accidentally by a Chinese cook who noticed that a substance called saltpeter glowed brightly when he accidentally spilled it into a fire. The earliest fireworks were made by pouring gunpowder into bamboo stems. When set alight, they exploded with a bang!

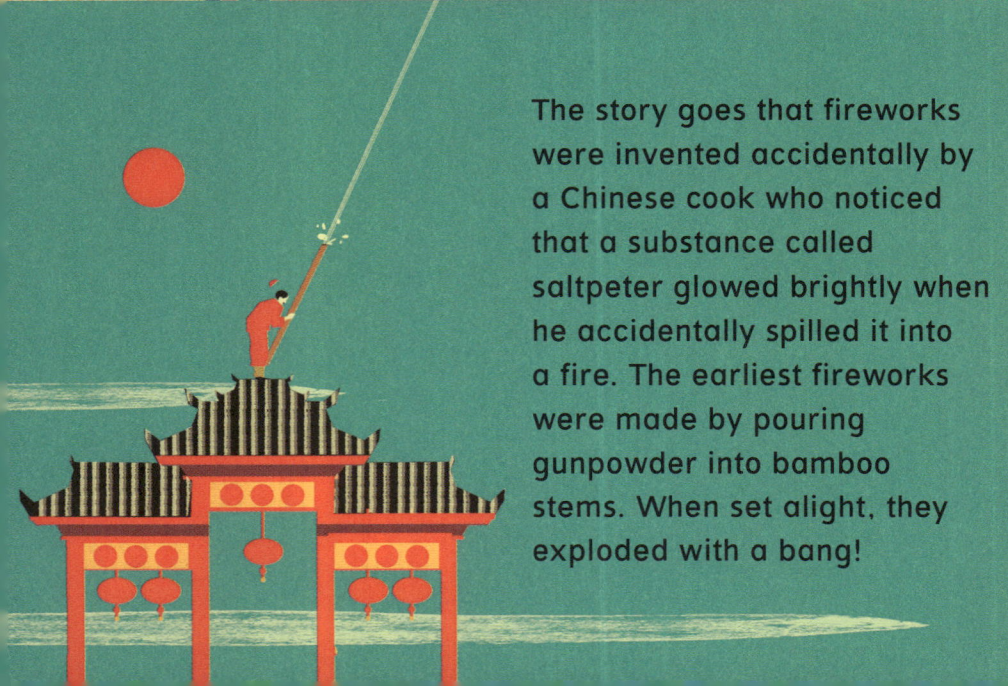

The most familiar element found in fireworks is sodium (Na). Table salt is sodium chloride, but sodium nitrate gives the festive explosions a yellow or gold colour. Like the other alkali metals (see pages 28-29), sodium is extremely reactive. It has to be stored in oil because it ignites on contact with water.

Barium (Ba) is responsible for green fireworks, in the form of barium monochloride. Lighter green colours come from barium nitrate. Barium is an alkaline earth metal (see pages 30-31) that gets its name from the Greek word *barys* meaning 'heavy'. It is used in a barium meal – an X-ray test that shows a doctor your insides.

Rich red fireworks are made of a salt called strontium carbonate. The element strontium (Sr) is named after Strontian, a village in Scotland where it was first discovered. About five per cent of all the strontium in the world is used in fireworks. You'll also find it in glow-in-the-dark toys and special toothpaste for sensitive teeth.

Travel

Your distant ancestors may have spent their entire lives in the same village, but now you can jump on an aeroplane or step aboard a boat and reach all corners of the globe. Thanks to our clever use of the elements it has never been easier to travel the world by land, air and sea.

There are over a billion bicycles in the world – one for every seven people. Nearly half of them are in China, the country with the highest population on the planet. A bike needs to be strong and also lightweight, particularly racing bikes used by professional cyclists. One option is to make the frame out of scandium (Sc), a silvery-white metal, which is often mixed into an alloy with aluminium.

There are over 10,000 planes in the sky at any one time, which means a lot of metal above your head! A jumbo jet is made of over 50 tonnes of the light, strong metal aluminium (Al). The jet engines on most aeroplanes contain blades called turbines, which spin at incredibly high speeds to create propulsion. These blades are one of the biggest uses of the transition metal rhenium (Re) thanks to its ability to withstand temperatures of more than 3,000°C.

Even underwater transport makes clever use of the periodic table. Like aeroplanes, submarines need to be lightweight, but also strong enough to withstand the huge pressure of all the water pressing down on it. The Russian Navy build some of their submarines from titanium (Ti) because its strength allows them to dive much deeper than those built of other materials.

The Future of the Elements

The way we use the elements in the periodic table needs to drastically change, and fast. It is no longer possible to burn fossil fuels, or mine for precious metals without having a serious impact on the environment. The planet is already warming up far too fast, and without urgent action our lives will be altered forever. Thankfully, humans have a history of coming up with ingenious solutions to difficult problems.

We need to generate a lot more of our energy from RENEWABLE SOURCES such as wind, solar and water power. Neodymium (Nd) magnets are used to run wind turbines, tellurium (Te) is crucial to solar panels and hydrogen (H) could fuel future environmentally friendly aircraft.

In France and China, giant machines called **TOKAMAKS** are under construction. **They will copy the way the Sun makes energy – the process of fusing atoms together known as fusion**, in a trial that could one day see a full-scale power station that creates clean, green electricity. Tokamaks work via magnetic fields which trap hot material inside a huge, hollow chamber and force it together to release energy. The special magnets used for this purpose are made of **niobium-tin** and **niobium-titanium**.

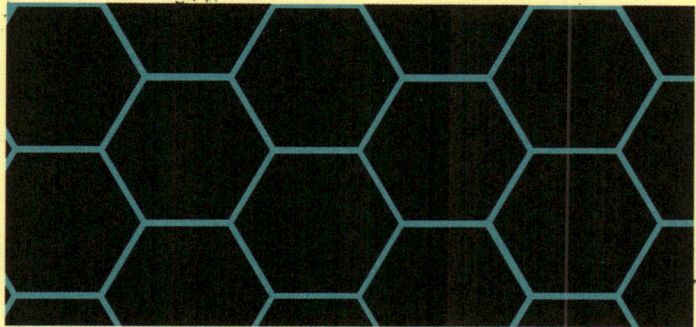

Our world could also be revolutionised in other ways, by using familiar elements in unfamiliar ways to create amazing new technology. **GRAPHENE** is one exciting material, **made from a layer of carbon shaped like a honeycomb and is just one atom thick**. That makes it super-lightweight, but also incredibly strong. Potential uses include tiny, cell-sized medical robots swimming inside your body and a computer tablet that you could roll up like a newspaper.

We are going to need to find more clever ways like this to make the most out of the periodic table if we want to continue to grow and expand as a species without polluting the planet. Can you help by becoming a scientist or engineer in the future?

Element 119 and Beyond

In 2019, the periodic table celebrated its 150th birthday. But how many elements exist? And how far does the table go? Scientists have discovered a staggering five new superheavy elements since 2000, and many suspect there are more to come.

SUPERHEAVY

PARTICLE ACCELERATOR

1. A beam atom is fired towards a target atom at one-tenth the speed of light.

beam atom

2. A beam atom crashes into a target atom sitting on a thin foil.

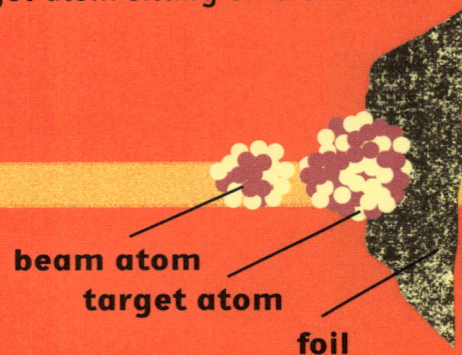

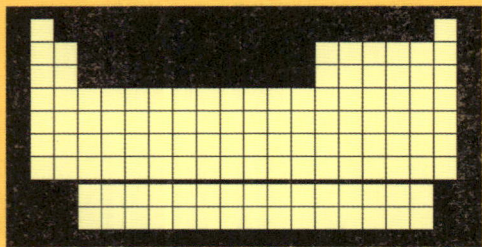

beam atom
target atom
foil

In March 2019, the ribbon was cut to mark the opening of the Superheavy Element Factory (SHEF) in Russia. It contains a particle accelerator ten times more powerful than any before, and it will be used to hunt for elements 119 and 120. Nuclear physicist YURI OGANESSIAN (see page 53) leads the team of scientists at SHEF.

Like the elements recently discovered, these new elements will probably only last for a blink of an eye before disappearing again. But some scientists believe we are heading for 'THE ISLAND OF STABILITY' – an uncharted part of the periodic table where superheavy elements don't decay so fast, making them as stable as many of the lighter elements. It may be they already occur naturally, but in such small amounts that we haven't found one yet.

ELEMENT FACTORY

3. If fusion occurs, the new superheavy atom flies through the foil. The extra beam atoms are separated.

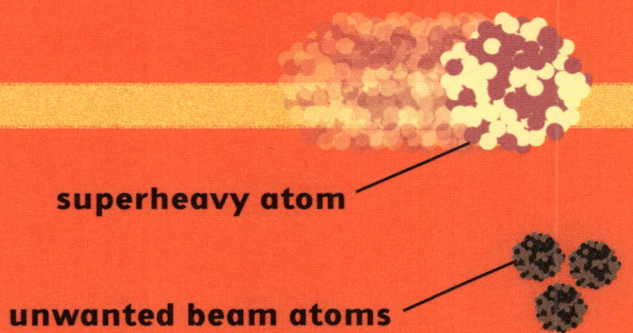

superheavy atom

unwanted beam atoms

4. The superheavy atom lands on the detector. It begins to decay, releasing alpha particles, which are detected. This tells scientists what element the atom is.

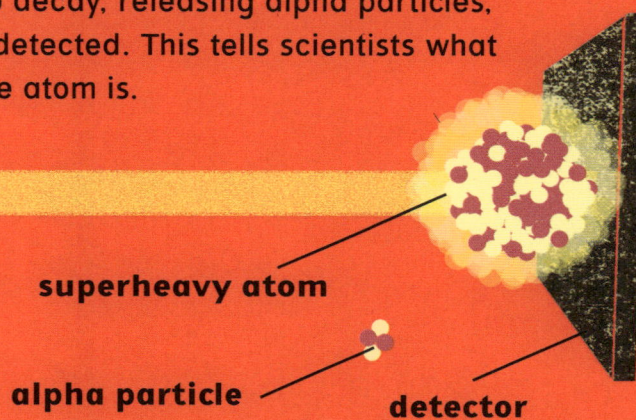

superheavy atom

alpha particle

detector

New element discoveries would extend the table into the eighth row for the first time. Stable super-heavy elements could have unusual and game-changing properties. The periodic table may yet have more extraordinary elements up its sleeve. . . and perhaps you might play a part in discovering more of its secrets.

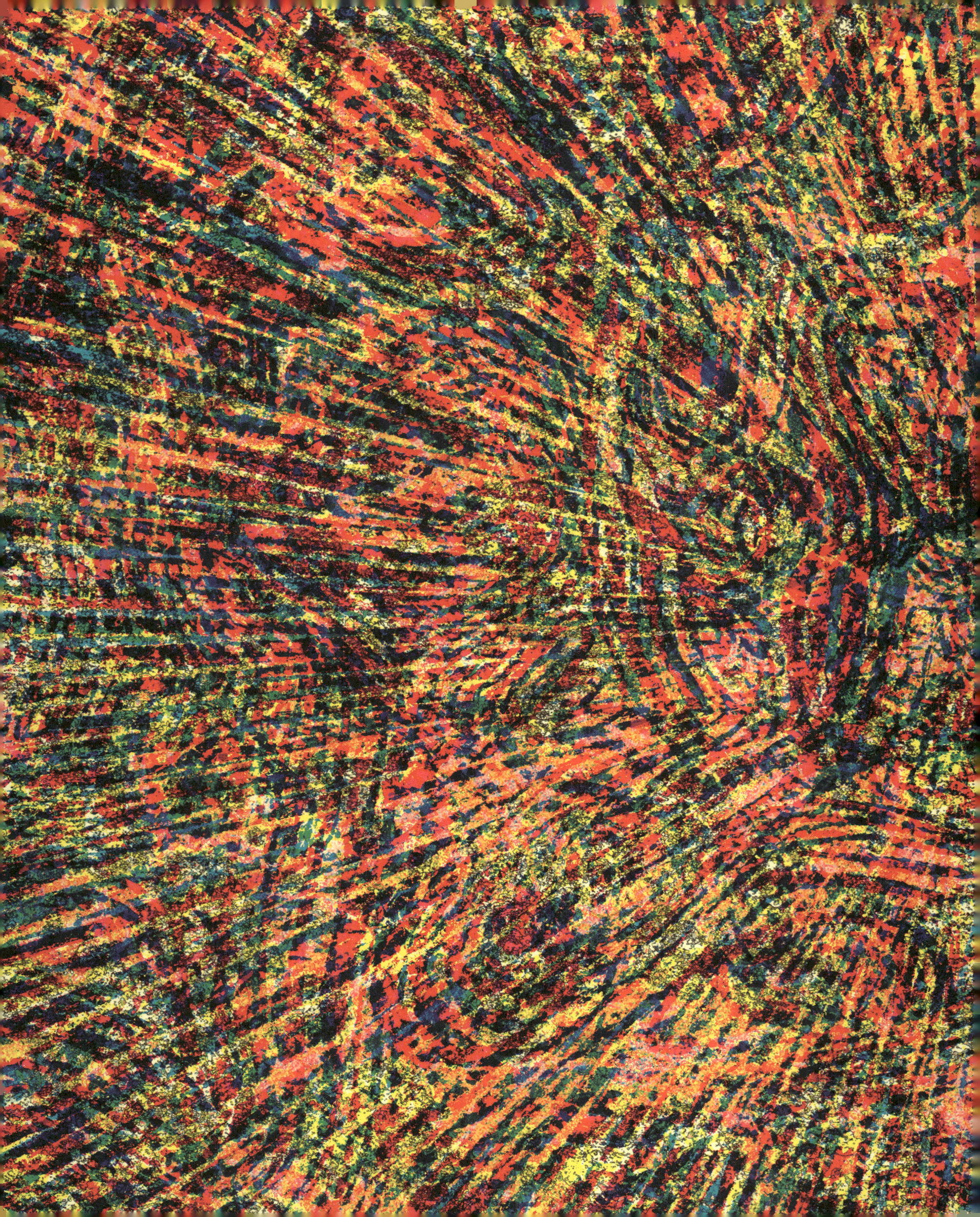